Merry Christmas
2021

Love,
Jimmy & Amy

"In *The Wisdom of Faith*, Coach Bobby Bowden gives us something we all desperately need but can never seem to find— wisdom. But not just any wisdom. He gives us the kind of wisdom that can only be found in a man whose life has been devoted to faithfulness and the fear of the Lord. I'm so thankful he wrote this book, and I know that his practical and sensible words will echo for generations to come."

—Matt Carter, Pastor of Preaching,
Austin Stone Community Church, coauthor of *The Real Win*

"This is the personal dimension of my father that few have had the chance to see. We children saw it growing up. And we've seen it ever since. He does not change when he is in the public eye. His words and demeanor have always been guided by one overarching aim: to follow the path of Christ wherever it leads. This book reveals what he discovered along the way."

—Tommy Bowden, former coach at
Clemson, Tulane, Auburn, Alabama, Kentucky,
and Florida State, a featured analyst on FOX Sports
South as well as an SEC and ACC analyst on
Raycom Sports, and author of *Winning Character*

"I was fortunate enough to break into the business of college football under Coach Bobby Bowden. Coach Bowden's conviction of his faith was instrumental to me in coming to know Christ, the greatest decision I made in my life thanks to his example and guidance. *The Wisdom of Faith* will bless many readers, just as I've been blessed by Coach Bowden's ministry."

—Coach Mark Richt, head football coach
at the University of Georgia

"I am proud to have been Bobby's friend for fifty-seven years, and this book reminds me there is only one Bobby Bowden. This book is a written masterpiece directly from his heart and soul. A must-read for all."

—Lee Corso, featured football analyst
on ESPN's College Gameday

"I'm a huge fan of Coach Bowden for a number of reasons: his honesty, integrity, and the passion he has for what he does. Like most coaches, he wants to share his winning ways with others not to boast but to teach, the winningest coach in Division-1 FBS has all those real life experiences to draw from. Whether he's roaming the sidelines at a Florida State football game or in the locker room with his team, coach is a man of faith and practices what he preaches! A great read by a great man, can't put it down!"

—Darrell Waltrip, winner of eight-four career
NASCAR Sprint Cup Series (TM) races and
a three-time champion, lead analyst for NASCAR on
FOX, and coauthor of *The Race*

"One of the greatest football coaches of our time takes his readers on a journey through the ups and downs, defeats and victories that have made up his life, and revealed the one thing that has gotten him through it all, his unshakable faith in God."

—Charlie Daniels, country music legend
and member of the Grand Ole Opry

"There is nothing like getting a peek into the life of a godly man. You will be inspired by Bobby's stories and wisdom. He lets us into a life that has been well-lived."

—Darrin Patrick, lead pastor of The Journey,
Vice President of Acts 29, chaplain to the St. Louis Cardinals,
and author of *The Dude's Guide to Manhood*

"Coach Bowden gives us insight into the role his strong faith in God has played in his life. He continues to coach as he reveals his game plan for victorious living."

—Sylvester Croom, one of first black athletes at University of Alabama, first black head coach in the SEC (Mississippi State), and current running backs coach of NFL's Tennessee Titans

"Coach Bobby Bowden in his new book, *Wisdom of Faith*, shares his insights as to what real victory looks like as we walk this journey of life. While he has led teams to national championships and is admired by coaches and fans across the nation, his greatest success is in living out the wisdom he has gained through the trials and tragedies of life. His story is one that will encourage all of us who depend on Christ and seek His wisdom to do this life well."

—Les Steckel, President/CEO, Fellowship of Christian Athletes

THE WISDOM
of FAITH

THE WISDOM
of FAITH

BOBBY
BOWDEN

with Steve Bowden

B&H
PUBLISHING GROUP
NASHVILLE, TENNESSEE

978-1-4336-8451-7

Published by B&H Publishing Group

Nashville, Tennessee

Dewey Decimal Classification: 234.2

Subject Heading: FAITH \ CHRISTIAN LIFE

2 3 4 5 6 7 8 • 18 17 16 15 14

This book is dedicated to my wife Ann and to the family we created together.

God startled me with a grace unimagined when I first saw Ann. Her family had just moved to town. They bought a house on the corner about five blocks from me. She was only fourteen. I was almost three years older. She joined the church I attended and immediately enlisted for duty in the adult choir. No one asked her to be in the choir. Who asks a fifteen-year-old to sing alongside a bunch of gray-headed people? But that was Ann's way. She didn't wait to be asked. And she didn't care that she might be too young. If she was in, she was all in. That's what membership meant to her. She was quite a girl. I noticed her from the back pew. That's where my buddies and I sat to get away from our parents. It's where all teenagers sit when they get the chance. Except for Ann. She was different. She never noticed me as she sang. But I sure noticed her. I couldn't take my eyes off her.

Sixty-five years later, I can attest that she has not changed. She is such a driven woman. All of my success has been guided by her determination. I never made—or wanted to make—any important career decision without her input. She had insights I lacked. And a wisdom that helped shape my role as a husband, father, grandparent, friend, and coach.

I also dedicate this book to my children and their families. They already know the thoughts contained in its pages. What was passed down to me from my parents is now passing through my children to the fourth and fifth generation. Kinship is a powerful bond . . . a covenant relationship that does not require signatures. Their love and loyalty have enriched me beyond measure.

ACKNOWLEDGMENTS

I wish to thank B&H Publishing for their encouragement and diligence in making this book a reality. Lots of people want to write a book. It takes a good publisher and editor to make that happen. But it's not just them. A host of their colleagues work in the background, their hands also on the clay, helping to shape and mold it into what it was meant to be. In Scripture, when a gathering of people was too numerous to count, the authors used the word *multitude*. In regard to B&H, I truly am indebted to a multitude. They are many, and they work in unison, like the muscles needed to create a single heartbeat. Such has been my experience with B&H. If I started naming names, I would mess it up. They know who they are. And they know what their skills have enabled. I am in their debt.

I also wish to thank my oldest son, Steve, who has helped clarify my thoughts for publication and put my words on the page. He was given access to decades of notes I have accumulated, and verses of Scripture that shaped my worldview, along with thoughts and quotes and other scribblings that struck me as insightful over the years. We discussed them for hours. And reflected on them. I shared my further thoughts and told him what should be said. He rendered my words into the book you hold now. Steve has an advantage over most. Like his brothers and sisters, he knows me from the ground up. So he became my scrivener. It makes for less editing on my part.

CONTENTS

Introduction: The Wisdom of Faith   1

Chapter 1: The Wisdom of Fear   7

Chapter 2: The Wisdom of Trust   17

Chapter 3: The Wisdom of Courage   31

Chapter 4: The Wisdom of Responsibility   45

Chapter 5: The Wisdom of Humility   65

Chapter 6: The Wisdom of Patience   89

Chapter 7: The Wisdom of Discipline   113

Chapter 8: The Wisdom of Contentment   131

Chapter 9: The Wisdom of Suffering   153

Chapter 10: The Wisdom of Love   185

Epilogue   205

THE WISDOM
of FAITH

*Eat honey, my son, for it is good, and the honeycomb
is sweet to your palate; realize that wisdom is
the same for you. If you find it, you will have a future,
and your hope will never fade.*

(Prov. 24:13–14)

On a cloudy afternoon in September 2004, as the outer bands of Hurricane Frances approached the Florida Gulf Coast, my son-in-law and grandchild were killed in a car accident. They were on their way to my grandson's football practice. The storm was tracking northward across Florida. At last report it was centered near Tampa, a couple hundred miles

1

to the south, too far away to be a danger but close enough to make one wary. Or so we thought. An unexpected gust of wind caused the accident. On the interstate just west of Tallahassee, the wind blew their car into the right-hand lane, where they locked bumpers with the car beside them. They broke free but swerved across the median after losing control. A utility vehicle from Gulf Power Company was in the opposite lane, heading southeast toward Tampa to provide relief for those in harm's way. It happened on a Sunday. We buried them on Thursday. I don't recall much in-between.

On Friday I flew south to Miami with my football team for the FSU-Miami game. The morning after the game, as my wife and I sat in the Miami airport, the death of John and Bowden were still heavy on my mind. My wife Ann and I would have swapped our lives for theirs. Any parent would. I know my daughter Ginger would. And her husband's parents would. But that option was not offered to any of us. As we sat waiting to board the plane, I opened my notebook and penned a letter to my six children. I wrote it for my sake as much as theirs, a reminder of what I've staked my life on for more than eighty years.

With their permission, I share it with you:

7/10/04 (Miami Hilton Airport-10:05 A.M.)

My Dear Children,

When the TRAGEDY occured Last week I saw again the Bond of Love our Family Has for each other. I witnessed the inner strength of Ginger in a time of mortal crisis And the Love of Her mother, Brothers, Sisters, spouses, Nephews, Nieces, Children As well As in laws & Friends. Oh, How I Love All of you!

This Brought BACK the memory of when you were just Children And your Mother would Stay up Half the Nite each Saturday Ironing & polishing your shoes. She would Lay your clothes out systematically & we would go the church each Sunday morning. Now is A good time to reflect on where you came From. Ann & My Number one goal was that we raise you in the Same environment we were raised. I remember vididly the Day you Accepted the Lord & were Baptized.

The good News of the TRAGEDy is that John & Bowden were saved & Today Live Again in presence of God in their New Heavenly Home. It has Been said that when we Die we can take nothing of ours with us, except ..... our children! Great Job, Ginger!

Keep in mind, At this time, our Family will Be together forever, if we All TRUST in Jesus & Surrender our Lives to Him. I Don't mean change Jobs or school, etc But just Make your Life Available to Christ As your GRAND Parents did And Ann And I Have tried to Do.

When I Die & go to Heaven (I Know I will) If All of you & your Family Are not there with me, when your time comes, I will Consider myself to have Failed in life. All the statues, Trophies, Championships etc will Be in vain. Somewhere Along the Line, I Failed you, if you are not there.

Now is the Time to recommit our Lives to Christ Just As you Did As A Child. Jesus said.... "I Am the Way, the Truth & the Life ... No man Comes to the Father except thru me", I Choose Jesus As my Saviour & Commit to Him!

EACH Night, This is my fervent Prayer.

Love,

Dad

3

Life is fired at us point-blank. We rarely have time to pause and say, "Wait! I'm not ready. Give me time to prepare." About the time we think we know what the day will bring, we realize we don't. Life is such a mystery. Like when a fog rolls in during a night at sea. We think we know what's out there, but not for sure. Our lights penetrate only so far. What lies beyond can be known only by sailing into the darkness, peering into it as best we can and watching vigilantly. We hear a sound on the wind. It is God's voice. He says, "Trust Me. Follow My voice. Come this way." And with all my heart, that's what I want to do. I do not resent the fog and darkness. Rather, I'm thankful for the voice that guides my path.

As I have done for many years, I rise each morning before 5:00 a.m. It's dark outside. My wife is asleep and the newspaper won't arrive until daybreak. I go to the kitchen and brew a cup of coffee. In past years, I ate a cookie or piece of toast for breakfast. These days, it's just coffee. One cup. Black. Then I read the Bible. I peruse a Bible commentary for insight and read a devotional passage or two. Bible verses such as "love your neighbor" are easy to understand but "judge not that you be not judged" seems to require a theologian. So I read what the scholars have to say. Then I pray. The world around me is quiet. No traffic on the road in front of my house. No birds chirping. Even the crickets are silent. To sit alone on the cusp of dawn is like witnessing creation. I close my eyes and seek my Creator. I ask Him to accept me as I am . . . to make me a better servant . . . strengthen me and make me wiser today than I was yesterday.

I need wisdom. With each passing day, I want it more. Over the course of eight decades, I've learned that wisdom and faith go hand in hand. If I trust God, He will give me understanding and strengthen me for His purpose. I come closer to seeing the world as He sees it, and with it comes a clearer vision of what I must say or do. Such a simple thought, yet so difficult. To have wisdom, I first must trust God. And obey. That fact has never changed. So I pray in earnest that God will give me insight and make me wise. I have no other choice. The sun will rise whether I want it to or not. Life will make its demands.

O Lord, please keep me off the path of fools. That road is wide and crowded. Yours is narrow. Grant me wisdom as I head toward the fork in the road.

CHAPTER 1

THE WISDOM
of FEAR

The fear of the LORD is the beginning of wisdom;
all who follow His instructions have good insight.
(Ps. 111:10)

When I was a child, I feared many things.

In the late 1930s, during the height of the Great Depression, my grandfather's construction business went bust and he moved in with us. I was little. He and I shared a bedroom. Shortly thereafter, my aunt and uncle moved in. Times were difficult. I feared what might happen if my parents lost the house. Where would we live? How would we eat?

Several years later in 1943, I was stricken with rheumatic fever. I wasn't allowed out of bed for six months. Rheumatic fever attacks the heart. The doctor wasn't sure how badly mine was damaged. Diagnostic tools were limited in those days, at least by today's standards. I was told that I could not play football again or engage in strenuous activity. Privately, the doctor warned my parents about the possibility of death. Even as a teenager, you think about things when you are bedridden. The dread of not doing the things you love most, for example, and fear of the unknown.

During those months in bed I listened to the radio. A brutal war raged across Europe, North Africa, Asia, and the South Pacific. Allied forces threw themselves against the powers of the Axis. Thousands of soldiers died each day, some of them not much older than me. Radio reports came in daily. In the Pacific, it was Pearl Harbor, Guam, Wake Island, and the ferocious Battle of Midway. In Europe, the German attack on Stalingrad, the battle for Tripoli, and the Warsaw Ghetto Uprising. I drew pictures of airplanes engaged in dogfights. I feared Nazis and the Japanese Imperial Army.

I feared other things too, such as the switch my mother used to remedy my misbehavior. The look in my father's eye also could be fearsome, though he was never heavy-handed. He was a cheerful, fun-loving guy who enjoyed people and practical jokes. My mother was gracious and even-tempered. But when I tested their patience, they taught me that discipline is a virtue every child should learn.

As I got older, I came to appreciate the fact that some fears are legitimate and should not be ignored. Fear can keep us off the wrong roads. It can help us avoid avoidable mistakes. Foolish errors are not worth repeating. Fear is the reminder.

In a practical sense, fear is a signal that something is amiss. It inspires vigilance and discernment. And wisdom essentially is the ability to discern what is edifying from what is harmful, what is safe from what is dangerous.

The Bible makes an even more dramatic claim about fear. It insists that wisdom itself is dependent upon fear. But only in regard to one particular fear . . . a fear that puts all other fears in perspective. That fear is "the fear of the LORD."

From a biblical standpoint, fear of the Lord is not merely *a* starting point on the path to wisdom. It is *the* starting point, the exclusive starting point. Those who want wisdom must first fear the Lord.

This mantra is repeated often in the pages of Scripture. Listen:

> He said to mankind, "The fear of the Lord is this: wisdom. And to turn from evil is understanding."
> (Job 28:28)

> Then you will understand the fear of the Lord and discover the knowledge of God. (Prov. 2:5)

> "The fear of the LORD is the beginning of wisdom, and the knowledge of the Holy One is understanding." (Prov. 9:10)

> The fear of the LORD is the beginning of knowledge; fools despise wisdom and discipline. (Prov. 1:7)

> Don't consider yourself to be wise; fear the LORD and turn away from evil. (Prov. 3:7)

> Don't abandon wisdom, and she will watch over
> you; love her, and she will guard you. Wisdom is
> supreme—so get wisdom. And whatever else you
> get, get understanding. (Prov. 4:6–7)

Let me offer my layman's explanation of what lies behind these words.

We all have a hunger for purpose and meaning. We want to live well and be happy and find that our lives matter. But how do we find it? What's the best course to follow?

Even if we never consciously ask those questions, we find ourselves on a journey in search of the answer. We hunger for something that we cannot quite put our finger on. We wake up each day and get dressed and head out the door in pursuit of it. Yet with each step forward, and with each passing day, we sense that we are getting no closer to finding it.

To see this illustrated in everyday life, I look at individuals who have achieved the very things most of us strive for.

In the realm of football, I think of Tom Landry. He happens to be one of the finest and wisest Christian men I have known who also happened to coach football. Tom played college ball at the University of Texas in the 1940s and later played professional football with the New York Giants. He eventually became the head coach of the Dallas Cowboys, where he remained for twenty-nine years. What a career! In addition to twenty consecutive winning seasons with the Cowboys, he won thirteen divisional titles, led his team to the championship game ten times in a seventeen-year period, and won two Super Bowl titles. He achieved a level of success that younger coaches like me dreamed about. His Dallas Cowboys came to be known as "America's Team." And you know what he found when he got to the top? After all those years of success? After having set records that may never be matched?

"Nothing," he said. "I found nothing."

All those achievements over the course of a lifetime—which certainly were well deserved—did not translate into happiness and fulfillment. That may come as a surprise to some, but it didn't surprise Tom Landry. His message to us other coaches was simple and straightforward: "Coach football because you love it. Work hard. Study the game. Do your best. But realize that there is no *there*, there."

He wasn't expecting anything more from football than to give it his best. For what he sought most deeply from life, he turned to God and found it.

Tom Brady, the great quarterback of the New England Patriots, echoed a similar sentiment about what one finds atop the pinnacle. After winning his third Super Bowl ring he appeared on TV and was asked to comment on his incredible success. As best I recall, he looked at the ring on his finger and said, "Why do I have three rings and still think there's got to be more? This can't be what it's cracked up to be."

A word to the wise, indeed.

Others reached the pinnacle of their profession only to be devastated by what they found. Celebrities, athletes, investors, developers, CEOs, politicians, trust-fund babies—people of all stripes and backgrounds who had it all and enjoyed the admiration of countless people who wanted the same—reached the top and were overwhelmed by the emptiness they found. Some turned to drugs and alcohol to dull the pain of discovery. Others used a bullet to the head. It can be a dreadful thing to find so little when one has so much.

When you're headed down the wrong road, it ultimately doesn't matter how fascinating the scenery is; you still end up in the middle of nowhere. I'm not complaining about success and the benefits that come with it. I have known my share of success and have seen the benefits. But I can affirm what Tom Landry, Tom Brady, and a host of others have said—namely, if you think your heart's deepest desire can be wrung from worldly success, you are in for a devastating disappointment. Riches can be more deceptive than poverty when you realize that neither can fill the deepest longings of your soul.

Most people do not live in front of a camera or in the public eye. Rarely do they have the opportunity to sniff at material wealth or celebrity or national renown. They are the vast swath of humanity, their days filled with work and family, neighbors and civic duties. They, too, wrestle with the enigma of life. The nagging question nips at their heels: *What's the point of life? I'm exhausted. When does happiness kick in?* Frustration builds as we run out of solutions. It is the human condition.

We want to get someplace in life but we're not sure where to go or how to get there. We climb pinnacle after pinnacle, only to discover there is no *there,* there. About the time we think we've arrived, we haven't. And more often than not, we prove to be our own worst enemies. The apostle Paul described his own experience in a letter to the church in Rome:

> For I do not understand what I am doing, because
> I do not practice what I want to do, but I do what
> I hate. . . . For the desire to do what is good is with

me, but there is no ability to do it. For I do not do
the good that I want to do, but I practice the evil
that I do not want to do. Now if I do what I do
not want, I am no longer the one doing it, but it is
the sin that lives in me. So I discover this principle:
When I want to do what is good, evil is with me.
(Rom. 7:15, 18–21)

So what does this have to do with the fear of the Lord?

When we meet the Living God, our lives are called into question at a deep and fundamental level. We are forced to admit that we cannot fill the void in our own lives, much less fill the void in others. We hurry through life as if we're in a rush for the end, yet never sure why we rush. Our way of living isn't working as planned. Our best efforts have proven feeble and insignificant. God forces us to own up to our failure. It is a crushing and helpless realization . . . one that God hardwired into our genes.

The French philosopher Blaise Pascal said that within each human being is a God-shaped void. The author of Ecclesiastes phrased it differently but meant the same, "He has also set eternity in the hearts of men" (Eccl. 3:11 NIV).

Such is the unease of life. We live restlessly, driven by an elusive hunger. We fill the God-shaped void with all kinds of substitutes, some good and some bad. They offer short-term relief but never really satisfy. Even the worst among us find some meaning in life, twisted though the efforts may be. Most find happiness in family, friends, service to others, and personal achievement. But nowhere along the way do we find the life we intended for ourselves. The troubling void remains. It is intense at some moments, faint in others, but always lurking.

Some go on a feeding frenzy to fill the void. Others give in to malaise or surrender to cynicism. Egos get involved. The farther we head down the wrong road, the louder we proclaim we know exactly where we're going. But we don't.

God knows the emptiness that drives us. He created it. He alone can fill it. It's by design. Here is His admonition to us, as simple as it is humiliating: "You do not have because you do not ask" (James 4:2).

The statement is an indictment of our fatal flaw. We ask for lots of things. We usually don't hesitate to ask for what we want. But we neglect to ask the most important question of all, namely, "What do You require of me?"

The question is a game changer. It's what makes God fearsome. We can't have it our way and His way. We can have if we ask, but only on His terms. That's the whole point of conversion. The word *conversion* means to turn and walk in a new direction— different from the path we've been following, a different style of life than we've been living.

The Living God cannot be tamed or domesticated. He is not a house pet. He does not bend to our will or bark upon demand. Nor is He the person next door who welcomes us to the neighborhood with a Bundt cake and a smile. God is more like a lightning bolt—good but dangerous. He fills the darkness of our lives with a brilliant and terrible light. Fools reach out to own Him and get the shock of their lives. The wise live in His light and give thanks. A reverent thanks. Fear and trembling are their signs of respect.

Such is the biblical testimony of those who encounter Him:

> I tremble in awe of You; I fear Your judgments.
> (Ps. 119:120)

Yahweh, if You considered sins, Lord, who could stand? But with You there is forgiveness, so that You may be revered. (Ps. 130:3–4)

Because they hated knowledge, didn't choose to fear the LORD, were not interested in my counsel, and rejected all my correction, they will eat the fruit of their way and be glutted with their own schemes. (Prov. 1:29–31)

My son, if you accept my words and store up my commands within you, listening closely to wisdom and directing your heart to understanding; furthermore, if you call out to insight and lift your voice to understanding, if you seek it like silver and search for it like hidden treasure, then you will understand the fear of the LORD and discover the knowledge of God. (Prov. 2:1–5)

There will be times of security for you—a storehouse of salvation, wisdom, and knowledge. The fear of the LORD is Zion's treasure. (Isa. 33:6)

"I will give them one heart and one way so that for their good and for the good of their descendants after them, they will fear Me always. I will make an everlasting covenant with them: I will never turn away from doing good to them, and I will put fear of Me in their hearts so they will never again turn away from Me." (Jer. 32:39–40)

One lives in God's presence in awe and reverence. He presses in upon us at every moment, impinging, interrupting, judging our failures yet offering peace and fulfillment in a new direction . . . His direction. We are His creation. We are designed to find happiness only according to His purposes. If we wish to walk away, He will allow it. The consequences will be ours alone to bear. That, too, is a fearsome power. He will let us walk into oblivion. Yet if we choose to hear Him, He will fill the aching void. God's love is fearsome. Those who understand are set on the path to wisdom.

> "The fear of the LORD is the beginning of wisdom."
> (Prov. 9:10)

CHAPTER 2

THE WISDOM
of TRUST

Israel, out looking for a place to rest,
met God out looking for them.
(Jer. 31:3 *The Message*)

One day Moses was in the countryside tending his father-in-law's sheep. It wasn't the best job in the world, but it put food on the table. Mutton, mostly. Off in the distance he saw a bush on fire. He watched for a while. Something wasn't right. Curiosity got the best of him, so he walked closer. Sure enough the bush was ablaze. Yet the fire did not consume it. He crept up until he was near enough to feel it. The sensation was eerie. Something was amiss. The hair on his neck began to

THE WISDOM OF FAITH

rise. Then came a voice from the fire, calling him by name. The encounter went something like this:

"Moses, I have a job for you. You must go to Egypt and tell Pharaoh to let My people go."

"Yeah, right," said Moses. "You're a hoot."

He peered around the bush, looking for his brother-in-law, a guy known for practical jokes. The flames leapt up and singed Moses's eyebrows. A second flash toasted his cheeks. Now convinced of his mistake, he turned aside and hid his eyes and trembled.

"But Lord," he pleaded. "Egypt? Me? In Pharaoh's court? That's like visiting Mecca with a Star of David on my forehead."

"You're getting ahead of yourself," the Lord replied.

"Can I at least tell them who sent me?"

"Tell them YAHWEH sends you."

"Huh?"

"YAHWEH."

"I am that I am?" Moses stammered. "That's not a name. It's a statement. And not a clear one at that."

"YAHWEH is all you need to know," boomed the voice within the fire.

"That you 'ARE'?"

"Yes, that I AM."

"You think they'll buy it?"

"You do not need another name!" God bellowed. "I am known by My deeds! Now go. Tell your kinsmen who are in bondage what I have told you. I will show them as I have shown you, as I showed Abraham, Isaac, and Jacob long ago. Then they will know I AM."

Here are the actual words:

> God replied to Moses, "I AM WHO I AM. This is
> what you are to say to the Israelites: I AM has sent
> me to you. . . . Yahweh, the God of your fathers, the
> God of Abraham, the God of Isaac, and the God of
> Jacob, has sent me to you. This is My name forever;
> this is how I am to be remembered in every genera-
> tion." (Exod. 3:14–15)

So Moses went. You can read about it in the book of Exodus. My point is that he went with newfound assurance. He had just encountered the reason for being. Not merely for himself, but for everyone, everything, including his ancestors. The discovery was more than comforting. He felt emboldened. Empowered. Like a man on fire. History itself belonged to YAHWEH. Nothing lay beyond His reach. Not that Moses realized it at the time. But he would soon enough. Trust would be the glue that bound them together, same as it was for Abraham, Isaac, and Jacob in the days before they knew the name YAHWEH.

I wish more kids today knew Bible stories. They teach great lessons. So does life.

For a period during my childhood, I slept in the basement of our two-bedroom home in Birmingham, Alabama. The space had been furnished with a comfortable little bed, but at night the room was dark and quiet. Like most kids, I was scared of the dark. Being cut off from my parents upstairs stoked fears of vulnerability . . . and my imagination. Who knew what monsters writhed beneath the bed . . . what faces might peer through the window? What was to stop them from seizing me in the darkness? Some nights the fear was overwhelming. I felt helpless and would cry out to my parents. A moment later, the door at the top of the stairs would open and my father would call down, "Bobby! Be quiet and go to sleep!" It was his no-nonsense voice. Authoritative and firm. What mattered most was that he heard me and responded. It reassured me. I didn't see him on those nights, except maybe his shadow against the wall when the light was at his back, but his voice was clear. I knew that *he was*. It was all I needed to know. His voice conquered the darkness and let me sleep.

That was decades ago. Many decades. I have long since become a man and aged. Dark nights have come aplenty during that time—dark days too. Only one voice counts in the end. *I AM*. I have heard it many times. He is the Living God. The God of Abraham, Isaac, Jacob, and Moses. And of Bobby Bowden. I put my trust in Him long ago.

My father died of an aneurism much too early in life. I had just turned forty and was not ready to lose him. In his last months, he lay comatose in a hospital bed almost as long as I was in bed as his child with rheumatic fever. In those final days, I took his hand in mine and told him I was the new head coach at West Virginia University. I wanted him to understand. I'm not sure he did. His passing broke my heart. I wish every father could be like him. His name was Bob Pearce Bowden—a name he filled with robust and contagious enthusiasm. Several years later my mother died also. She was named Sunset, after the heroine of a French novel that enchanted my grandmother while she was pregnant with my mother. Or so I was told. Some people got confused by my mother's name and called her Sunshine. She never seemed to mind. I loved them dearly. My only sibling, an older sister named Marion, died shortly before my mother. Then it was only me. My turn to be the voice at the top of the stairs. Could I be that voice? Their voice? Dare I be?

I had six children of my own, four more than my parents had. When I coached at Samford University in the early 1960s, three of my boys had to sleep downstairs in the basement just like I did. There's nothing new under the sun in that regard. Over the past eighty years, I invited over three thousand boys to play college football for me. Most of those years I lived in Tallahassee. It was far from home for most of them. They were young and impressionable. I was their coach. I felt responsible. Would my voice carry to the bottom of the stairs?

Wisdom is never more needed than when your voice is what others depend on.

When it's our turn to be found trustworthy, we listen with new ears to those who have gone before. They have wisdom to share. Listen:

> But I trust in You, LORD; I say, "You are my God."
> The course of my life is in Your power. . . .
> (Ps. 31:14–15)

> How happy is the man who has put his trust in the
> LORD and has not turned to the proud or to those
> who run after lies! (Ps. 40:4)

> You will keep the mind that is dependent on You in
> perfect peace, for it is trusting in You. Trust in the
> LORD forever, because in Yah, the LORD, is an ever-
> lasting rock! (Isa. 26:3–4)

> "For I know the plans I have for you"—this is the
> LORD's declaration—"plans for your welfare, not for
> disaster, to give you a future and a hope. You will

call to Me and come and pray to Me, and I will listen to you. You will seek Me and find Me when you
search for Me with all your heart." (Jer. 29:11–13)

Don't worry about anything, but in everything,
through prayer and petition with thanksgiving, let
your requests be made known to God. And the
peace of God, which surpasses every thought, will
guard your hearts and minds in Christ Jesus.
(Phil. 4:6–7)

The ancient Hebrews didn't sit around meditating on God. He was not an abstraction to be contemplated. Rather, He was a force to be reckoned with. They lived with God much like we live with our family and neighbors. They hoped, pleaded, rebelled, loved, hated, fought, anguished, and conceded. Trust is deeply personal. It is active and full of energy. And sometimes exhausting. So it is with the Living God. He can and will be contentious. We are the ones who provoke it, not Him. He wants what is best. He demands it. But in the end they found Him always to be steadfast. It was a love undeserved just by its sheer constancy. So they learned to trust Him . . . learned that He could always be trusted . . . and from trust came wisdom.

When the Hebrews talked about trusting God, they frequently used the term *bittachon*. It is a colorful word. The root meaning conjures an image of leaning with all one's weight. The word is pregnant with seeds of wisdom.

Imagine leaning against a wall. On the other side is a roiling chasm. Perhaps in that depth are the gnashing teeth of your enemies. Or the prospect of failure. Financial collapse. The threat of heartache. A tragic loss. Endless mediocrity. Or simply a fear of the unknown. Whatever it may be, you know the threat is real. If the wall gives way, you spill into the abyss. The image swirls in your mind. That's what life comes to at times . . . desperate moments when we are exhausted, out of breath and out of options. We need rest. Our legs are weary. Our strength is gone. So we put our full weight against the wall. The boards groan under the burden. Yet they never give way. They hold us up in our time of need.

The Hebrews chose that image when they spoke of trusting God. It was a tried and tested term. *Bittachon*. Lean on Him. Lean with all your weight. He can hold you up. And He will. That's how they described it.

> The man who trusts in the LORD, whose confidence
> indeed is the LORD, is blessed. (Jer. 17:7)

> Trust in the LORD with all your heart. (Prov. 3:5)

> Trust in the LORD and do what is good. (Ps. 37:3)

I affirm these words with a lifetime of experience behind me. Listen to this admonition from Proverbs 3:5 (NIV):

> Trust in the LORD *with* all your *heart* and lean *not on*
> your *own understanding*. (italics added)

Note the warning not to lean on your own understanding. This is not a put-down of humankind, human kindness, or the virtue of self-reliance. Most of us are reliable. We have a sense of what is needed and we do it. But our resources are limited. If we lean on ourselves, we eventually discover that the wall won't hold.

What is true of us is true of everyone. None of us can lean too heavily on others. We try, but it doesn't work. Life is too weighty for our friends to bear. And their lives are too weighty for us. Someone always feels let down. It is no one's fault. None of us were meant to bear a weight that only God can handle. It is a feature of existence.

The apostle Paul said it best when he wrote to the church in Rome:

> What then are we to say about these things? If God
> is for us, who is against us? (Rom. 8:31)

That's what our ancestors discovered. Lean on Him with all your weight. With all your life. Only then will you know. Your next step will be a wise one.

The year 1974 was my fifth season as the head coach at West Virginia University. The previous year we had fallen to a lackluster 6–5 record. Better things were expected in '74. But as the season got underway, disaster unfolded in slow motion. We lost our quarterback to injury before the season even started. Then we lost our back-up quarterback and our opening game to the University of Richmond, a team the pundits expected us to beat. On top of additional injuries to other players, we had to start a freshman at quarterback. He had talent but no game experience or grasp of our offense. We hoped for the best, but the best didn't happen. We lost six of our first eight games. By the time we headed to Blacksburg, Virginia, for our final game against a rugged Virginia Tech team, our record was 3–7. It was pitiful. Embarrassing. The program seemed headed in the wrong direction despite our best efforts. Many of the fans lost confidence in me. I could hardly blame them. I was hung in effigy on campus. Banners called for my ouster. The local media added fuel to the fire. I would be lying if I said it didn't trouble me. All those people can't be wrong. Maybe head coaching at the Division I level was too big a job for me. Maybe I didn't have it—whatever the *it* is we refer to when we say, "That guy has it, he has what it takes." All kinds of things go through your head as you watch the wheels fall off. Yet who could I complain to? After all, I was the guy in charge of this disaster.

I talked with the University President, James G. Harlow, on several occasions during that season. He seemed to understand the handicaps we were strapped with. Yet he was catching as much heat as I was.

A few disgruntled people went too far. One threw a steel brick into the front door of our home. Another set off a cherry bomb in the mailbox, and yet another poured a bucket of blue paint on the family car. They all operated at night under cover of darkness. The worst was when some guy called our house on several occasions and said he saw my youngest daughter walk home from grade school in the afternoons and was going to "get her." It was a death threat, my first as a coach.

Such troublesome misfits are a fraction of every community. They reflect on no one but themselves. My children loved West Virginia. So did my wife and I. We left many friends there when I took the job at Florida State University (FSU) in 1976.

My point, though, is that I was at the lowest moment of my career when our team arrived in Blacksburg, Virginia, that Friday night. We checked into our hotel rooms and settled in. I met with the coaches and made plans for game day. Then I went to my room. The light on the phone was flashing. There was a message. It was from the University President. James Harlow wanted to talk. I wasn't surprised by his call. It had been a terrible season. Time for it to end, I figured. I knew he understood the problems we faced, but who could blame him? I was as disappointed as anyone. So I headed out the door to meet with him. It was time to man up.

"Bobby," he said when we met, "I wanted to let you know I talked with the Board of Regents. We regret that things have not worked out well this season. It's not been good in a lot of ways. Anyway, we want you to know that . . . we are behind you one hundred percent."

That may not be an exact quote, but it's the gist of our conversation.

God comes to us in many guises. When you have no more to give, someone appears and bears your weight. They hold you up. All you can do in response is rest for a moment upon the strength of their word and return to the battle, emboldened. It is a hint, a reminder, of what God asks us to do with Him.

As an aside, let me tell you about the game we played the next day. As the clock wound down in the fourth quarter, we led Virginia Tech 22–20. A major upset was in the making. They had the ball with time running out, but Virginia Tech ran a wishbone offense that was time consuming, and the clock was ticking away. They had the ball on their side of the field, a long way from field goal territory. They ran a play. We stopped them. The referee threw a flag on our defense, a fifteen-yard penalty for some infraction or another. I was livid and made sure the referee knew it. He apparently didn't like my tone. That drew a second fifteen-yard penalty. Thirty yards of penalties from out of nowhere, it seemed, and with time running out. It put them in our territory in range of a field goal. They plowed forward, but our defense held them on third down at our own fifteen-yard line. We made a gallant effort. At least they didn't get a touchdown out of it. So now came fourth down.

The field goal attempt was hardly more than a chip shot. They sent in their kicker. A week earlier this guy kicked a fifty-four yarder to beat Florida State in the closing seconds. We had studied the film and knew what he could do. He was good. The writing was on the wall. Nonetheless, the frustration of a losing season seemed to inspire our defense. They took their stances before the snap of the ball, their backs arched, their muscles taut and ready. When the ball was snapped they bulled forward through the offensive line and threw out a hand and blocked the field-goal attempt. I wish I could remember whose hand it was. The ball careened sideways and WVU fans erupted with delight. What a finish to a hard-fought game. The weight of the world seemed lifted off my shoulders. But wait! There was a flag on the ground. The umpire announced that Virginia Tech's center had snapped the ball before the signal was given to resume play. The play had to be repeated.

Talk about having all the strength sucked out of you. There are moments when it seems God is sending a message, and not a welcomed one. "There is a place you fit in," God seemed to say, "but this is not it. Coaching isn't your gig. At least not head coaching."

When I heard the field umpire say the play must be repeated, I saw the entire season unfold in a split second. Maybe you've had a similar experience. You want to throw your hands up and say, "Yep, this about says it all. The critics got it right. I'm clearly not meant for the job."

But the words of WVU's President were still fresh. "We're behind you one hundred percent," he said. I looked out on the field, saw my players who had given all that was in them to give, and thought to myself, *Let them make the kick. It's just a game. We'll get our injured players healed in the off-season and start fresh next year.*

The ball was snapped. Our defensive line, though exhausted, took a deep, hungry breath and surged forward with all the strength left in them. But Virginia Tech was ready. They bowed up and refused to allow penetration. The kicker made his move . . . the same precise move he had made a thousand times in practice. You could hear his foot thump into the ball. Upwards it went toward the goal posts. It took less than two seconds. Then I heard the cheers. It was our fans, not theirs. The kick had missed the mark. Time expired. We won the game 22–20.

Go figure.

You can draw whatever conclusions you want from the end of this story. It seems worth telling. For my part, I can give you a hint of God by citing the confidence I felt when President Harlow told me, "We are behind you one hundred percent." The weight of that entire football season—a weight borne by me, my coaches, the players, and all the fans who supported WVU football—was not too much for him to bear. His trust meant more to me than any other experience I had as a young head football coach.

That next year we went on to a 9–3 season and beat North Carolina State in the Peach Bowl. It wasn't much by some standards. But it meant the world to me. Lou Holtz was the opposing coach. His record speaks for itself. I've accomplished quite a few things in the aftermath of President Harlow's vote of confidence.

He bore the weight of an enormous burden. If he was still alive, I would tell him to his face. Someday I will.

As for wisdom?

Trust the voice in the burning bush.

"I AM," He announces. "Be still and know that I am God."

Bushes burn everywhere for those with eyes to see.

CHAPTER 3

THE WISDOM
of COURAGE

"Haven't I commanded you: be strong and courageous?
Do not be afraid or discouraged, for the LORD
your God is with you wherever you go."

(Josh. 1:9)

C ourage is a critical virtue in the arsenal of faith.

The greatest tests we face in life are not tests of intelligence but tests of character. Every character trait needed for wise living, whether it involves loving-kindness, patience, humility, honesty, discipline, standing up for what is right, or simply holding one's tongue will be tested time and again. Knowing the right thing is the easy part. Doing it is what's difficult, especially when such action may cost us dearly. That's why courage is essential. Our quality of life depends on our capacity to live courageously.

Courage comes to us as a gift from God, freely given. Like everything related to the Living God, it is tinged with mystery and borne from the assurance that *HE IS*. Those who discover such inner strength know that it comes from a source beyond themselves.

Since childhood I have been fascinated by the stories of World War II. Over the decades I have read many books on the subject. Hundreds of them. Sometimes twenty a year. They fill the shelves in my study. I heard the stories unfold in real time on the radio in the 1940s, which makes reading the details so fascinating. I was nine years old when the war broke out. There were no televisions in those days, only radios. My imagination filled in the gaps. I would lay in bed listening to popular shows—Bob Hope, Jack Benny, and Red Skelton, the big band music of Benny Goodman and Artie Shaw, the crooning of Bing Crosby and the Mills Brothers—when suddenly the voice would break in: "We interrupt this program . . ."

You knew right off it was an update on the war. Somewhere in Europe or Asia a tough battle had just been fought. A major offensive was launched. The enemy, we hoped and prayed, had just suffered a stinging defeat. Oh, how I pictured the heroism of our men in battle. Blood-and-Guts Patton hitting them hard and making it hurt. MacArthur taking Bataan like he promised. Eisenhower and Montgomery moving soldiers around like master chessmen. None of our guys in the field wanted this war. War is hell. But once you're in it, you fight to win. Otherwise you live with a boot on your neck.

I am amazed by the courage of soldiers who risk their lives to save others. War produces men and women like that. Some take the risk and live to tell about it. Others die trying. Their tales of valor are inspiring. A harrowing moment arises on the battlefield, for instance, when one's comrades are trapped by the enemy in a deadly attack, with no escape and little chance to survive. Other soldiers can see the dilemma but are powerless to help. To attempt a rescue would require running into the teeth of a withering hail of bullets, completely exposed and without cover or protection. The situation is hopeless. Instinct says to retreat, fall back to a safer position and fight from there. But a different instinct takes hold in the hero. All he knows is that if he runs away from his friends, he runs away from himself as well . . . straight into the arms of a life not worth having. Whatever hope remains for those trapped soldiers, whatever chance they have for survival, somehow depends on him. Their hopes and fears mysteriously become his own hopes and fears. He feels the burden. He identifies with it. His survival and their survival become one and the same. If he abandons them now, he abandons something essential to his own life, something so essential that death itself is not too great a price to pay. So he grips his weapon and rushes into the maelstrom . . . into the teeth of enemy gunfire and a likely death, driven only by the imperative to *do something that seems necessary*. Many a young man made that decision in World War II. They do it still today. Ironically, the decision is never a complicated one but is always difficult to explain. When those who survived their ordeals were later asked why they did it, most shrugged and answered: "It had to be done. If not me, then who?"

It had to be done? Really?

Who would have scolded the hero for holding back? Certainly not those who ran in the opposite direction. Prudence advises us to escape when the challenge is too great . . . take the safe route . . . live to fight another day. A young man with a lifetime ahead of him has no obligation to confront impossible odds.

Or does he?

Some obligations defy words. They arise at a moment's notice and strike us with the force of an inner imperative. We don't always choose the moment. Sometimes the moment chooses us. A conviction arises similar to what the young Martin Luther expressed when he stood before Emperor Charles V in 1521—knowing that he might well be arrested and executed for his blasphemous insistence on the priesthood of the individual believer. Luther had been critical of the Church, accusing it of gross excesses. In effect, he challenged the authority of the entire religious hierarchy in Europe at that time, insisting that believers had direct access to God in a way that didn't require ecclesiastical intermediaries. Political and religious officials who called the meeting expected Luther to stand before them and apologize, humbly confessing that his beliefs were mistaken. They wielded the power of life and death. There was no court of appeals. They expected Luther to cower in fear and seek forgiveness. Instead, true to his convictions, he rose and boldly stated: "Here I stand. I can do no other. God help me." From such courage was born the Protestant and Catholic reformation. Four hundred years later in the Battle of Iwo Jima during World War II, Medal of Honor recipient Jack Lucas and his buddies were ducking bullets on the front line when a couple of grenades landed in their foxhole. There wasn't time to pick them up and throw them out. Lucas quickly pushed the two grenades together, put his helmet on top of them and then curled over the helmet. If he couldn't live, at least his buddies might. Seconds later the grenades exploded. His buddies survived the blast. Miraculously, Lucas did, too, though he spent the rest of his life with over two hundred shell fragments in his body.

I don't cite these examples to suggest that courage requires the sacrifice of one's life. Far from it, even on the battlefield. Heroic acts are not suicide missions. Sacrificing one's life might just as easily be stupid or foolish, depending on the circumstance. An act can be courageous without anyone being harmed. The issue is not the risk of physical death but rather the higher good that lays claim to our lives and the risk we take to have it. That higher good is what gives life its meaning. It gives us a life worth living for . . . and dying for. When we are willing to lose ourselves in order to have that life, we discover life as God intended us to know it. That's the lesson battle heroes teach us.

Jesus of Nazareth came to this conclusion in regard to His own life. He knew it was risky to stay true to the Living God. Resolving privately to do God's will is one thing. Standing publicly for God is another issue entirely. Not that He was aiming to get caught in the crosshairs of public opinion, but He could see the problems ahead. Tough times require tough decisions. The matter weighed heavily on His heart. Such thoughts were in the background when He said to His disciples:

> "For what does it benefit a man to gain the whole
> world yet lose his life?" (Mark 8:36)

You can feel the burden of His question. He put it to Himself as much as to the disciples who followed Him. God's will was His inner imperative. It wouldn't be easy. It never is when the stakes are high. He challenged those around Him to trust God the way He did . . . to try and see the world through God's eyes rather than their own. When one looks with God's eyes, a pathway appears. It's not the same path that we have chosen. It's a new path. Heading in a different direction. It's also daunting. Dangerous. Not because God designed it that way, but because human sinfulness—yours and mine as much as anyone's—has made the journey perilous. God knows the direction we must go. But to follow His path, we first must give up on ours. That's what Jesus had in mind when He motioned for everyone to listen.

> Summoning the crowd along with His disciples, He said to them, "If anyone wants to be My follower, he must deny himself, take up his cross, and follow Me. For whoever wants to save his life will lose it, but whoever loses his life because of Me and the gospel will save it." (Mark 8:34–35)

The context of Jesus' statement is revealing. The location was a place called Caesarea Philippi, the equivalent of modern-day Las Vegas. Fun City, a magnet for locals who craved excitement and an escape from the drudgery of life. Caesarea Philippi is where you go when life has lost its luster and you need a reason for being. Against this backdrop, Jesus posed a question to His disciples. He asked:

"Who do you say that I am?"

Peter spoke for all of them when he answered:

"You are the Messiah!" (Mark 8:29)

His acknowledgment represented a "eureka moment" for the disciples. It dawned on them as never before that Jesus of Nazareth might be the real deal. His message resonated. He seemed headed in a direction much more interesting than any place they had been before, including Caesarea Philippi. Perhaps He could fulfill their hopes. Judas hoped to rid the world of pagan idolatries. Peter hoped for something to believe in, John something to love, and Thomas something certain. They remind me of Dorothy's friends in their quest for the Wizard of Oz. Each searched for what was missing in his life. But none of them had yet gone far enough in the quest for a life worth having.

That's when Jesus dropped the hammer:

> "For whoever wants to save his life will lose it, but
> whoever loses his life because of Me and the gospel
> will save it." (Mark 8:35)

When we come to see the world as God sees it, we realize that we will not always end up in happy places. Evil is real. Battles must be fought. Lessons must be learned and sacrifices made. Character is forged on the anvil of conflict. And courage is essential. Such courage comes only from God. That was Jesus' conviction. He dared to follow the Living God. That's what led Him to Jerusalem and the cross. When He arrived in the capital city, things got ugly, just as He anticipated. Yet still He trusted God, even to the end. The world fell silent when Pontius Pilate arrested Him and nailed Him to a cross. It seemed that heaven fell silent too. Jesus' defeat was swift and decisive. He was no match for the power of Rome. The disciples themselves were in a panic, more frightened of life now than in the days before they met Jesus. How stupid they felt. How foolish. What an awful thing to be caught duped and naked on the stage of life. Then the Living God answered. It happened two days after Jesus was killed, on a Sunday morning. Peter visited the grave on Sunday just after daybreak. He found the stone rolled away. The tomb was empty. Along the shores of Galilee some days later, at a place where the disciples had fled for safety, Jesus appeared. He held out His hands and showed them the wounds . . . and the power of the Living God.

What we are willing to lose defines what we are enabled to have. It's a conundrum, I know, especially in this day of terrorism when desperate people sacrifice their lives for causes that entirely miss the point, if only because they brutalize the innocent, dehumanizing and killing civilians in senseless acts of violence. Such acts represent not the redemption of human suffering but rather the cheapening of it. Jesus saw life differently. Harlots and tax collectors wanted the good life as much as anyone. Only, they looked in the wrong places, same as the disciples who followed Him and the Romans who crucified Him. It is to self that we should die. It is for God that we should live. On this journey all are invited but none should be forced. That's where the terrorists get it wrong. Killing noncombatants to make a political or religious point is not courageous. It is folly. A cruel and shameful folly, brutal and wasteful and pointless. Such killing takes but does not give. Its heartache is not what God desires. Governments and individuals are both to blame. Jesus makes a higher claim. The death He speaks of is really about living, or rather, how we are set free to live once we encounter the Living God. Here's how He expressed it on another occasion:

"Again, the kingdom of heaven is like a merchant
in search of fine pearls. When he found one price-
less pearl, he went and sold everything he had, and
bought it." (Matt. 13:45–46)

In this light we begin to understand how Jesus looked at the
world. When His eyes fell on Jerusalem in those final days, this
was His foremost thought . . . the pearl of great price. It is the
wellspring of courage.

Simply put, those who surrender to the Living God begin to
value themselves and others and all of creation in a new light.
The old way of valuing things changes. We think of ourselves
differently. We look at others differently. Our priorities change.
Even death itself, once the abysmal curtain call on all we hoped
for and loved, loses its powerful grip. The apostle Paul spoke of
his own experience—in tones both joyous and liberating—when
he proclaimed to the believers in Corinth:

Death, where is your victory? Death, where is your
sting? . . . But thanks be to God, who gives us the
victory through our Lord Jesus Christ! Therefore,
my dear brothers, be steadfast, immovable, always
excelling in the Lord's work, knowing that your
labor in the Lord is not in vain. (1 Cor. 15:55,
57–58)

Paul speaks with a courage that runs bone deep. He didn't discover such courage in himself. He would be the first to insist that
it comes from God alone. His great source of power came through
the risen Christ, who confronted him on the road to Damascus
and opened his eyes to the Living God. Through Christ he found

an unconquerable strength that he never before had known. Thus
he wrote:

> Who can separate us from the love of Christ? Can
> affliction or anguish or persecution or famine or
> nakedness or danger or sword? As it is written:
> Because of You we are being put to death all day
> long; we are counted as sheep to be slaughtered.
> No, in all these things we are more than victorious
> through Him who loved us. For I am persuaded
> that not even death or life, angels or rulers, things
> present or things to come, hostile powers, height
> or depth, or any other created thing will have the
> power to separate us from the love of God that is in
> Christ Jesus our Lord! (Rom. 8:35–39)

Take that thought with you into the next tough challenge you
face. Dare to believe it and watch what happens. What do I mean
by *dare to believe*? This: Be honest . . . stand up for what is right
. . . do so with humility . . . bite your tongue when needed . . .
resist the temptation to do evil . . . dare to see the world as God
sees it and live according to His will. And then discover how God
will strengthen you for each challenge you face. The Living God
is never idle. He puts His strength in us to do His will. Trust Him
and see for yourself.

When I started out as a coach in the 1950s, I didn't understand how demanding it would be to stick to my convictions. The
world was fresh and invigorating in those early days. Few people
knew my name. The biggest pressure on me to win was the pressure I put on myself. Keeping the courage of my convictions was
fairly easy.

Some years later, I found myself the head coach of a very successful program whose teams were in the spotlight constantly. The landscape changed. We played high-profile games around the country. A national audience watched us on Saturdays and read about us on weekdays. Florida State football was all over the sports news. With such exposure came scrutiny and criticism as never before. One of the issues that drew frequent criticism was the way I treated my players. There was a public perception that I was a lax disciplinarian who held a cavalier attitude toward player misbehavior. I doubt any of my players or coaches would agree with that assessment—either in my early years or my later ones—but the perception existed nonetheless. For my part, I had long ago resolved to treat my players as I would want another coach to treat my sons. It was a decision I made early in my coaching career, when I was old enough to think of players as my sons. I stuck with it for the rest of my career. If a player makes a mistake, get the facts straight and then administer a punishment that seems fitting. There are lots of ways to do that, from running him up and down the stadium steps at 5:00 a.m. to taking away his cafeteria or dormitory privileges. Such punishments matter to college kids. If he makes too big a mistake, or too many, dismiss him from the team. But always treat him as though he is your child.

As I got older, that approach seemed more and more like the right way to handle things, so I stuck with it despite protests from the outside. My players were young men with lots of physical talent. They had more temptations thrown at them than the normal student. They were held to high standards in the public eye. All rightfully so. But those players also were typical young people. I resolved to see them the way I thought God saw them, the way I tried to see my own sons at that age. My players were not just young men with talent. They were my boys. My sons. Their well-being had been entrusted to me by their parents. If they needed punishment, I preferred to do it out of the public eye, where only coaches and fellow teammates would know. Sometimes that wasn't possible—such as when a player had to sit out for several games or else be dismissed from the team—but I no more wanted to humiliate a player in public than a parent would in regard to his or her own child. Unfortunately, that formula got me in trouble with some fans and journalists over the years. Some people enjoy the spectacle of a person being humiliated in public. Others wanted proof that I had been sufficiently harsh. What they didn't understand was that my orders came from God, as best I understood it, and not from the public. If my style was deemed inadequate, they could get rid of me and bring in someone with a different style. For my part, right or wrong, I did what I believed God wanted.

I decided long ago that God ultimately is the One I must please. If others disagree with my treatment of players, so be it. My job is to ask God for wisdom and rely on Him to guide me. He helped me stick to my guns and not run from the fight. Whatever courage I found in life came from God. He has proven too faithful for me to turn from Him now.

I am convinced that the courage we most need in life comes only from the Living God. To know Him is to discover an inner strength that otherwise we will not find in ourselves. Like other virtues, courage can be nurtured and helped to grow. Those who want to live courageous lives are advised to begin with the little things—occasions to face challenges and do the right thing when we're at work or home or out with friends. Doing the little things well improves our strength and confidence. The more we practice, the better we get. By the time larger crises set in, we have formed habits of courage that are like a second nature.

I suspect everyone who lives courageously on a daily basis received guidance from others earlier in life. I think of a child climbing the ladder to the top of the slide. The parent is right there, holding the child's hand until the child is not just able—but also willing—to climb the ladder and slide down without anyone's help. You can see the confidence grow. And with confidence comes improvisation. Next up is the jungle gym, or maybe a tree limb. Anything that involves climbing. Fear loses some of its grip. A world of possibility opens up. We all possess the power to help others become more courageous.

We do it by helping the weak become strong. The Bible tells us repeatedly to train our children in the ways of God. Daily courage—little-step decisions—can become habitual if we show our children how to do it. Parents are icons in a child's eye. Children imitate them. If we live courageously, our children will too. If we stand for what is right and good, oppose evil when we confront it, they will learn from us. They imitate God through us. We become mediators of the very courage we need in our own lives.

Pray for God's wisdom.

Rely on His teachings.

Dare to follow Him.

You soon will find yourself among those who are "more than victorious" through Him who strengthens us.

CHAPTER 4

THE WISDOM
of RESPONSIBILITY

When I was a child, I spoke like a child, I thought
like a child, I reasoned like a child. When I became
a man, I put aside childish things.

(1 Cor. 13:11)

If someone came to me and asked how they might gain wisdom, I would ask: "Are you willing to take full responsibility for your life?"

This is not the only question I would ask. Or even the most important one. But it is one of the first I would ask. The Bible has confronted me with it many times. It is a threshold question for anyone who seeks the wisdom of faith.

Why? Because if we will not focus the light of truth upon our-selves and own up to what we find—stop long enough to search ourselves and ask what we are doing with our lives and what we should be doing—we will not experience the profound way God can empower us for living.

Some do not answer *Yes* to the question—do not take full responsibility for their lives—until they steer into the center of a terrible storm. At that point all seems lost and there's no one else to blame. The only option is to fall on one's knees and cry in despair. Honesty sometimes is forced upon us by the sheer weight of our folly. Choices have consequences. Sometimes the cumula-tive weight of our bad decisions crushes all the joy and hope we have. Fortunately, many turn to the Living God in such moments and discover God's saving grace. Though their folly may cost them dearly, sometimes leaving scars that last a lifetime, their painful lessons become portals to the grace and wisdom of God.

I think of the Old Testament story of David. His youthful heroics catapulted him into the public limelight. He did what was needed time and again. He was courageous . . . a winner . . . a resourceful leader in battle . . . always leading the charge and brimming with youthful self-confidence. Who hadn't heard of the way he beat Goliath in battle with nothing more than a slingshot? Such bravado was the stuff from which legends are made. Israel wanted him as king. So they gave him the job. But power went to his head. A moral failure plagued him early on as Israel's leader. One day he saw a woman named Bathsheba that he wanted for himself. She was young and pretty. He was determined to have her. He learned that she was married to a soldier in the army . . . *his* army. And he reasoned that, as king, he was entitled to what he wanted. So he schemed with one of his generals to have

Bathsheba's husband killed in battle. The plan worked. Uriah died in battle and David took Bathsheba as his wife. But as so often happens with secrets, no one keeps them well. Word spread about the scheme and David's complicity in it. The prophet Nathan eventually heard about it—apparently from a reliable source. Filled with the wisdom of a righteous and angry God, Nathan asked to meet with David. At that meeting—by asking David to help him solve a riddle—he confronted David with the choices he had made and the man he had chosen to become. Here's the gist of Nathan's visit:

> The LORD sent Nathan to David. When he arrived, he said to him: There were two men in a certain city, one rich and the other poor. The rich man had a large number of sheep and cattle, but the poor man had nothing except one small ewe lamb that he had bought. He raised it, and it grew up, living with him and his children. It shared his meager food and drank from his cup; it slept in his arms, and it was like a daughter to him. Now a traveler came to the rich man, but the rich man could not bring himself to take one of his own sheep or cattle to prepare for the traveler who had come to him. Instead, he took the poor man's lamb and prepared it for his guest.
>
> David was infuriated with the man and said to Nathan: "As the LORD lives, the man who did this deserves to die! Because he has done this thing and shown no pity, he must pay four lambs for that lamb."
>
> Nathan replied to David, "You are the man!"
> (2 Sam. 12:1–7)

We are not told whether David owned up to his deeds in the presence of Nathan or instead rationalized his way out of taking full responsibility. Such rationalizations are usually a private matter, a way of escaping guilt and shame by dulling the edge on the sword of truth. Either way, it wasn't until the death of his rebellious son Absalom some years later that David finally fell to his knees. The death of his son was easily the most abysmal and painful moment of his life. Tragically, Absalom's rebelliousness resulted from strife within David's family, a strife that David himself had helped create over the years. The news of Absalom's death was devastating nonetheless. Absalom was his beloved child . . . flesh of his flesh and bone of his bones . . . more like him than any other of the children. He loved Absalom fiercely despite their bitter fighting. He gladly would have reconciled and thrown his arms around his child in peace and forgiveness. When the news arrived that Absalom was dead, David turned away from the messengers and dragged himself toward a private chamber to be alone with his grief, crying as he went. Nothing in life could have prepared him for this moment. The pathos in his voice is unmistakable to any parent:

> "My son Absalom! My son, my son Absalom! If only
> I had died instead of you, Absalom, my son, my
> son!" (2 Sam. 18:33)

David's folly cost him dearly in this case, a beloved and rebellious child. But his grief led him into the care of the Living God, in whom he found salvation enough both for himself and Absalom. He could accept that Absalom's destiny was in the hands of the Living God. His own fate rested there, as well. The heart of God is greater than anyone can understand. So is His power and grace. David's hope rested on that foundation.

At the other end of the spectrum are those who take responsibility for their lives early and often. The most difficult task of life—taking full responsibility for themselves and their choices—is a challenge they accept daily. Not that they manage every circumstance perfectly. No one does. But they aim to leave the world a better place than they found it. When they do make mistakes—or fail in some painful way—they look first at themselves, how they should have acted differently, and see that it is their responsibility to change the error of their ways. They are not strangers to guilt and shame. But they do not wallow in it. Or try to fix the blame on others. They learn from their errors and make improvements. In so doing, they raise the standard for all of us. We admire them. We see the wisdom of their ways.

Such people exist all around us. We usually don't read about them in newspapers or popular magazines because there are no salacious details to report. No embarrassing skeletons in the closet. No dirt worth dredging up. They are the backbone of every good family and every good community. Do they harbor regrets? Of course. Who doesn't? But their character is what stands out. People trust them. Admire them. Listen to them. And respect them. Some even fear them and try to bring them down. Such destructive efforts are to be expected. People of poor character do not appreciate a contrast to their own behavior. It's easier to drag others down. But most people sense that their own dignity is raised a notch by people of good character. Perhaps many notches. They show us what we have a right to expect from one another. More important, they show us what we should expect of ourselves. Our worth as human beings is somehow tied directly to this matter of personal responsibility. That's what people of good character reveal to us. And good character is fashioned on the anvil of responsibility.

The Bible doesn't address the matter of personal responsibility explicity. It simply assumes we are free and accountable. The story of Adam and Eve makes it clear. In Genesis 2—3, we read that God created Adam and Eve and put them in the Garden of Eden to tend and keep it. They were meant to enjoy fellowship with God and experience life as He intended it. Obedience to their Creator was the only ground rule. It was a choice the Creator allowed them to make. God's conversation with them went something like this (my paraphrase):

> I have set you in the midst of a beautiful Garden.
> I give you the power to name every animal, and
> whatever you name it, that is what it will be called.
> I give you the fruit of many trees and fresh water
> to quench your thirst. And I give you an environ-
> ment that is serene and secure and meant for your
> happiness.
>
> But I also give you one other thing. I give you
> freedom—some of My own power—so that you
> can make choices for yourselves. Let me warn you
> in advance. Freedom is dangerous. But the gift is
> worth giving. So listen to Me. Trust Me. Obey. Use
> your freedom as I have instructed and all the good-
> ness of Eden is yours. Otherwise, you will discover
> consequences you will not like. I'm the One who
> created this garden. I know how it must be tended.
> If you choose a different path, I will become your
> adversary. I will not let you ruin My creation.

Over there is a tree. Its fruit is forbidden of you
to eat. The tree stands as a reminder that freedom
entails responsibility. Enjoy all that I have given
you. But do not eat of that tree. Now go. Tend My
garden. Enjoy the life I bestowed upon you.

We know how the story ends. Adam and Eve chose to eat
from the forbidden tree. Freedom indeed is dangerous. I suspect
the fruit was ripe and pleasant to taste. Temptation usually comes
well packaged. Afterward they felt ashamed. What appeared
satisfying proved not to be. When the sound of God's approach
rustled through the leaves, their shame intensified. Nothing quite
does us in like the unsparing light of truth.

What makes this story relevant is its searching honesty—not
only in regard to our responsibility but also in regard to the
lengths we go to hide our irresponsibility. Listen to what happens
when Adam and Eve get called out.

Then the man and his wife heard the sound of the
LORD God walking in the garden at the time of the
evening breeze, and they hid themselves from the
LORD God among the trees of the garden. So the
LORD God called out to the man, and said to him,
"Where are you?" And he said, "I heard You in the
garden and I was afraid because I was naked, so I
hid." Then He asked, "Who told you that you were
naked? Did you eat from the tree that I commanded
you not to eat from?" Then the man replied, "The
woman You gave to be with me—she gave me some
fruit from the tree, and I ate." So the LORD God
asked the woman, "What is this you have done?"

And the woman said, "It was the serpent. He
deceived me, and I ate." (Gen. 3:8–13)

Shocker, right? Accusations flying in every direction. Adam
blames Eve. Eve blames the serpent. I'm amazed one of them
didn't get an eye poked out for all the finger-pointing that went
on. Of course, you and I have never done that, right? We would
never try to blame others for our own personal failures. Surely
Genesis 2—3 is just a story passed along by ancient people who
believed in myths. What does the Bible possibly know about my
life or yours?

We don't enjoy the light of truth because with it comes guilt
and shame. It's okay for God to walk through someone else's
garden. Shame on them if they haven't tended it well. Then God
shows up in our garden . . .

That happened to me one time. God showed up in my garden.
Actually, He has come many more times than one. But one occasion stands out in my memory. God confronted me in the guise of
a matronly grammar school teacher. The memory bears a striking
resemblance to the story of Adam and Eve.

Let me explain.

In 1944 I was in the eighth grade at Barrett Grammar School
in Birmingham. My teacher gave us a math test one day. She took
our tests home that night, graded them, and handed them back
the next day with her markups. If you had seen the results, you
would have thought my favorite color was red. I missed quite a
few. I knew my parents wouldn't be happy. Anxiety set in.

Our teacher had a practice of calling each student to her desk
to review our answers. She would give the entire class an assign-
ment, and during that time she met with us individually to go

over the mistakes we made on the test. It was her way of helping us improve. Before it was my turn, I changed one of my wrong answers. Then I walked up, handed her my test, and stood beside her as she looked it over. Seconds later, I noticed the change in her expression. She placed a finger on the spot I had edited and asked, "Did you change that?"

"No," I replied. I did my best to look sincere. She saw right through me.

She stared at me for a long, painful moment. But she said nothing. No follow-up questions. No accusations, just that penetrating stare. I didn't merely feel guilty for what I did. At a deeper level, I was ashamed. What I did was wrong. She and I both knew it. She couldn't prove it—an angle that didn't dawn on me at such a young and tender age—but then again, she didn't need to prove it. The look in her eye said it all. She knew the truth just as I did. Hers was more than a look of disapproval. I saw her disappointment too. Her opinion of me had changed. My lie seemed to hurt her as much as me. Yet she said nothing.

In later years I came to understand her look. I had similar experiences in dealing with my children, my employees, and my football players. What I later understood about that day in 1944 was that I didn't merely take a wrong answer and change it for my benefit. I took something from her as well. I took some of her willingness to trust me, some of her belief in my goodness. That eighth-grade experience was a minor incident. I don't wish to overdramatize or make too much of it. But the principle remains. In diminishing myself, I had diminished her as well. I had taken something from her . . . namely, her trust in me . . . and her trust in herself for trusting me. That was the pain in her eyes. Choices have a ripple effect. The failure to take responsibility for our lives—a failure of honesty and integrity—diminishes not only us but others as well.

I never saw that teacher again after the school year ended. I was off to high school and a new set of teachers. But I could not forget the look on her face. Or the truth she discovered about me. Life went on, of course. I finished high school, got married, had children, and started a coaching career. Life proved more weighty than an eighth-grade math test. But then again, maybe not. Every once in a while that old memory popped up. She never knew how much I regretted cheating her and myself that day. I never got comfortable with what she discovered. The memory was embarrassing. If she ever thought of me since then, what kind of person did she picture me to be?

Thirty years later, in 1973, I was the head football coach at West Virginia University. My name was in the news more than once. My wife and I travelled to Birmingham that summer to visit our families. We stopped at a restaurant and walked passed another older couple on their way out.

"Bobby Bowden!" one of them exclaimed. I looked up and immediately recognized my eighth-grade teacher. The unexpected encounter struck me like a lightning bolt. She appeared delighted to see me, eager to say hello after so many years. I could see it in her smile. But only one thought came to mind—that day in class thirty years earlier when I lied and she looked right through me. The words spilled out almost instantly:

"I did it!" I confessed. "I changed the answer!"

She had no idea what I was talking about. I explained and we laughed about it and chatted a moment longer before parting company. It sure felt good to get that off my chest. Even today, the memory remains instructive. In my confession (and her laughing acceptance) came a taste of grace. I was forgiven. That shameful moment was wiped away. Let me tell you, grace is needed in life and grace tastes good. It takes the sting out of failure. Undeserved though it is, grace lifts a mighty burden. It comes to us in a kind word. Or a forgetful laugh. Or some other gesture that signals all is forgiven. Grace heals. It makes us whole again.

I owe a great debt to my parents for setting an example for me in my youth. Most of the good in me—whatever there is of it—is owed to their influence. They made themselves available to God and became wonderful examples for me to emulate. Others played a role, too, such as my eighth-grade teacher. How did she know that a look was all I needed? How could she have been so wise? Maybe she felt more foolish than wise. I will never know. But I know God works in all things for good. The look on her face was a constant reminder of my need to improve and be a better person. Personal failure counts against us, but it can work for good. It spurs us to rise above ourselves . . . improve ourselves . . . and refuse to fall again into the same empty pit. Guilt and shame have a rightful place in the hierarchy of moral experience. But ultimately the stain is not removed until we are forgiven. That's why grace holds the highest place in matters of salvation. It is only through the grace of another that we can be washed clean. That's the lens through which Paul came to view our predicament:

> For all have sinned and fall short of the glory
> of God. They are justified freely by His grace
> through the redemption that is in Christ Jesus.
> (Rom. 3:23–24)

In a separate letter to the church in Ephesus, he comes back to this point again:

> For you are saved by grace through faith, and this is
> not from yourselves; it is God's gift. (Eph. 2:8)

Paul is as searchingly honest as those who told the story in Genesis. When we strip away all the excuses we create for ourselves—all the justifications for why we are who we are—the results are far from flattering. It is every person's predicament. Some are more honest about it than others. That's what I mean by taking personal responsibility for one's life. What others acknowledge about themselves is their decision. What we acknowledge about ourselves is up to us. The Living God wants to show us how to live. He comes bearing the gift of grace. To receive it, we first must experience the need of it.

Most of our unhappiness in life is self-inflicted—the result of choices we have made and continue to make. This realization is difficult to acknowledge. But it is true. No one forces us to do what we know is wrong. Or fly off the handle. Or shirk obligations. No one forces us to be discouraged, angry, jealous, greedy, resentful, dishonest, or desperate. Some wish to blame their problems on someone else. Their finger-pointing is dishonest and tiresome. Others acknowledge their personal flaws but with a "woe is me" tone of defeatism, as though change is impossible and misery inevitable. They cry out into the night with no expectation of an answer. God can change that. But first we must allow it. If we will not take possession of our lives—assume full responsibility for who we choose to become—we cannot discover the full measure of God's grace and power.

Life is difficult. No one doubts it. Difficulties are a given. But let's acknowledge that freedom of choice also is a given. We are free to choose how we react to whatever life throws at us. Think life is tough at age twenty? Or fifty? Try being my age. Life doesn't get easier after eighty. One set of challenges gets replaced by another. Complications always arise. Stairs, for instance. And pains that aren't familiar. Good grief, my memory is so bad that my wife wants me to hide my own Easter eggs next year!

Short of heaven, I don't know anyone who gets a pass on difficulties. Life's challenges come at different times and in different doses. How we choose to face those challenges is what makes the difference in life. Our response defines who we are. Great souls rise to the challenge. In God's eyes, we all have greatness written into our nature. He made us to be such persons. So why not choose greatness? He gives us a path to follow. He offers the strength we need. If only we would believe it. And trust Him. And do His will. That's what faith has taught me.

The apostle Paul gave all the credit to God for enabling him to become a new man. First, however, he had to give up on his old self. The old Paul, the one who was so angry and contemptuous and unforgiving, had to die. He had to own up to the person he had become and genuinely not want to be that person any longer. When he did that—when he experienced his profound need of the Living God—he found grace and acceptance and a life made new. Here's how he described the experience to his friends in Galatia:

> I have been crucified with Christ and I no longer
> live, but Christ lives in me. The life I now live in the
> body, I live by faith in the Son of God, who loved
> me and gave Himself for me. (Gal. 2:19–20)

Life in Christ was something Paul wanted each new day. It was Christ who empowered him. But it was Paul who chose Christ daily. Let me say that again. Paul had to choose every day. He had to wake up each morning and decide whether or not Christ's power would dwell in him. He chose to make it so . . . to make himself available to Christ. And he encouraged the believers in Galatia to do the same. He wanted them to continue forward with the decisions they made for Christ. Stick with it. See it through. Trust Him even more. Discover for themselves what Paul discovered in his own life. To take responsibility for one's life means not waiting around for something to happen; rather, it means choosing to let Christ live in you and make it happen. It is a deliberate decision . . . one we make daily until such decisions become habits and we settle into the lifestyle of the Living God.

In regard to our social responsibility, we must give our best to help make the world what God created it to be—full of goodness and love and the fullness of life. But the world is comprised of individuals, and so it is within each individual's life that God's saving work first must be done. We cannot help make the world more as our Creator intended until we first learn to see it through our Creator's eyes.

I hear the word *fairness* bandied about frequently these days. Many use the term, but few pause long enough to explain what they mean. I coached college football for almost six decades. Many of my second- and third-string players practiced as hard as the others and felt it was *unfair* that they weren't in the starting lineup. My children had similar complaints when they were young and their freedoms were restricted, same as I did as a child. So I'm always interested to hear someone else's opinion about what is fair and unfair.

When I hear TV pundits and some politicians talk about how unfair life is for certain people, the usual implication is that the unfairness is someone else's fault. And sometimes that is true. On too many occasions, however, unfairness is cited only as a way to excuse the behavior of the aggrieved party, no matter how reprehensible their behavior might be—as if to say, "How else can you expect them to act, given how unfairly they have been treated?" I get suspicious whenever I hear people use that word in exculpatory or self-serving ways. Or in self-pitying ways. It often comes across as a way of blaming one group while holding the other group completely blameless. Such talk is sometimes naïve and at other times sinister. The Bible has a lot to say about fools who make excuses for irresponsibility.

God takes a very strong stand against unfairness and injustice. Anyone who reads the Bible will discover as much. Prophets such as Amos and Jeremiah pronounced a scorching judgment upon governments and individuals who abused their power and trampled the poor underfoot. Nathan's confrontation with King David is but one example. Jesus echoed that same sentiment. The people of God are called to feed the hungry and clothe the naked and set free those who are oppressed. Genuine hardship— the kind that the needy have no ability to avoid and no way to improve—breaks the heart of all who know the Living God and see the world through His eyes. But let's tell the whole story, no matter how much it makes others wince. A great deal of human misery persists because individuals do not take responsibility for their lives. Bad things happen to good people. That sad truth has existed since the days of Job. But good people are never forced to live badly. If we surrender this point, we surrender something essential to the dignity and worth of every person, especially those who face hardship and are challenged to rise above it.

Not all of the suffering in our society has to do with unfairness or injustice. Many of the improvements needed require individuals to take responsibility for themselves. And much of our misfortune is the result of bad behavior that no one forced upon us. Change requires us to take responsibility for our lives no matter how "unfair" life is or has been imagined to be. Only then will we see things improve. We are fools if we evade this fact, whether for self-serving reasons or political motives or otherwise. And we are bigger fools if we exempt people from doing their rightful part to make their own lives better.

Some people don't seem inclined to improve their situation in life. I think of parents who don't seem to mind how late their children stay out . . . about the number of teenage pregnancies and births to single mothers . . . about the high school drop-out rate, the "knock-out" game, the misogynistic message behind much of rap culture, the myriad of violent video games, and the irresponsibility of so much that emanates from the entertainment industry—all of which contribute to the problem of irresponsibility.

I know how this sounds coming from an eighty-year-old guy. Things today aren't like they were in my childhood, so therefore things are worse. I get it. I don't suppose any generation of older adults has had a different sentiment when what once was familiar gives way to what is new. But the facts speak for themselves. A growing number of people feel that they are accountable to no one, and that every bad experience in life is someone else's fault or someone else's responsibility to fix. They look around for a serpent to blame. And others jump on the bandwagon. "Yes," they cry, "it's the serpent's fault. Let's find him." And they look around for a serpent who fits the bill. Sinners always feel better when they condone the sins of others. It's an easy way to justify one's own bad behavior. It's as if they say, "I won't blame you for your bad behavior if you don't blame me for mine." Codependence works well with sin. Together sinners look for a serpent who is anyone but themselves. The quest has a righteous feel to it. Like a crusade. A godlike and redemptive act. "We will find the evildoers and blame them." That's what Adam said. And Eve. Some stories never grow old.

People lose themselves whenever they lose sight of God. Such is the moral hazard of our age. And of every age. Those unwilling to be honest with themselves—who look for the speck in another person's eye but never take seriously the beam in their own—find it difficult to live in God's world. The Living God has ground rules. One of them is being honest with ourselves and with Him. Such honesty isn't possible until we take responsibility for who we choose to be. Short of that, wisdom is not possible.

Not that we can fix our lives by ourselves. Far from it. The deepest ailments in life cannot be fixed by anyone but God. In my youth, I watched Hitler try to fix Germany's problems according to his philosophy of life. So, too, Stalin in Russia and Mao in China. Later came Fidel Castro and Che Guevara and many others like them. Their visions failed. Sinners cannot fix the problem of sin, no matter how hard they try or how much power they wield. Indeed, they tend to make matters worse, if only because of their godlike zeal. None of them had a place for the Living God. Indeed, they mocked the idea. So much for them and their grand schemes. Will human history ever tire of such arrogance dressed in sheep's clothing?

At the other end of the spectrum, our Founding Fathers came up with a plan to limit the power that one sinful human can exert over another. They devised a constitutional republic that was dependent on individual liberty and a freely chosen faith in the Living God. They had no intentions of imposing a compulsory state-sponsored religion. Personal freedom meant too much to them. But they also knew that their new system of governance depended on citizens who lived responsibly. Faith in God was the glue that made it work. They promoted faith in God without establishing one sectarian group over another. They were opposed to the establishment of a theocracy. No sectarian group was to be given the political power to impose their views of God on everyone else. Their view of government and its limited powers was grounded in the biblical notion of human sin and our need to be protected from it. If all have sinned and fallen short of the glory of God, only a fool would put too much power in the hands of such people. We are now two hundred and fifty years into the bold experiment they undertook. How well it goes will be up to individuals and their willingness to assume responsibility for their lives. I doubt I will live to see the outcome of the project. Hopefully it will last for centuries to come. I like the founding principles. They are biblically based. In the lives of both individuals and nations, if God is to work in us, we must choose to let Him. No one of us, and no group among us, should be allowed to usurp an authority that belongs only to the Living God.

Our obligation to follow God's will is the only absolute in life. If we get that part right, the rest falls into place. Knowing God's will clears up the confusion. Doing God's will clears away the debris. The journey of life is satisfying when we know where to go and how to get there. I'm not saying that faith clears up every issue. Life is full of ambiguities. But life becomes less ambiguous when we allow the Living God to light our path.

One of the advantages of being my age is that I can look back over life and speak with more confidence than I could at age twenty. I've already made the journey that many are just starting. I'm familiar with life's twists and turns. I have the advantage of hindsight. With it comes clarity. Simply getting older helps. One learns things after years of trial and error. But experience of the Living God is what matters most. Looking back in faith, I can see how He works in the world and why He calls us to do His will. It makes more sense once enough years pass. Time may cloud our vision but not our insight. If your future is in front of you, take the next step wisely. A life awaits that you may never have suspected. Jesus' resurrection is the clue to where it leads.

How liberating to admit the truth and surrender! How empowering. Foibles no longer need defending. Hypocrisy goes by the wayside. The chance finally arrives for purity of heart. Truth alone is what matters. It is a difficult thing to do. The biggest obstacle is always ourselves. But afterward, we no longer swim against the current. The wearisome struggle ends. Moving forward in the truth is much easier than moving forward with lies, no matter what it costs. That's one of the ways God liberates us. He accepts our honest confession, demands that we do better, and empowers us to live in simple truth. I cannot explain it any differently than that.

Listen again to how Paul described his experience:

> I have been crucified with Christ and I no longer
> live, but Christ lives in me. The life I now live in the
> body, I live by faith in the Son of God, who loved
> me and gave Himself for me. (Gal. 2:19–20)

One must yield to understand. It doesn't guarantee that things will go smoothly all around. But your future will no longer be for others to decide. It will be for God to decide. Today may have been tumultuous. Now the day is ended. Turn tomorrow over to Him. And then sleep. Sleep is a good thing. We all need rest. God gives it to us freely if we will be honest about ourselves and trust Him. Praying in faith is the world's best sedative. Tell Him the truth. Not for His sake, but for yours. Then take what you find in yourself and entrust it to Him. His grace is boundless, His love fierce and unrelenting.

Listen to His voice:

> Now this is what the LORD says—the One who
> created you, Jacob, and the One who formed you,
> Israel—"Do not fear, for I have redeemed you; I
> have called you by your name; you are Mine."
> (Isa. 43:1)

Rest in Him and draw strength for tomorrow.
The Living God will guide us home.
Trust Him and see.

CHAPTER 5

THE WISDOM
of HUMILITY

When pride comes, disgrace follows,
but with humility comes wisdom.

(Prov. 11:2)

I am a sinner saved by grace.

I do not make this confession because others expect it. Or because I think it's proper to say. Or to impress you, the reader, with my religious credentials. I make the confession because it is a true rendering of my life experience.

Many of my contemporaries have offered similar testimony. They may use different words but their meaning is the same. Similar expressions echo through the pages of Scripture. They all are shorthand statements about the experience of God. It is a costly meeting.

Pride is what one loses in the encounter.

Humility is what one gains.

Pride is such a danger. Nothing in the history of humankind has caused more cruelty and crushed more spirits than pride. How many hundreds of millions—or billions—have perished beneath its sword, died in its prisons, starved in the fields of its greed, and cried out beneath the heel of its persecutions? The number is so large that we can hardly wrap our brains around it. Think of the Nazis who killed over six million Jews during World War II. Or Stalin and Mao with their millions more? How many murders does it take before counting no longer matters? Ten thousand? A thousand? Three?

Pride is the root of all transgression. Like a cancer it eventually destroys the host, but usually not before the sickness has metastasized and inflicted grief on others as well.

Pride—as the Bible speaks of it—is not the same as self-respect or the satisfaction one finds in honest achievement. I would hope every person possesses a healthy respect for their status as human beings. We possess a value established by God on the day of creation. Respect for oneself includes a respect for the obligations that go with being human, such as living with dignity, respecting the dignity of others, and holding ourselves and everyone else to the same moral standards.

But sometimes our view of ourselves gets overblown. We begin to think too highly of ourselves. Or of our opinions and achievements. Or else we quit holding ourselves to the standard we expect from others. It easily happens when flattery reaches a certain level. It works the same with power. Or wealth. But it can happen also with those who have no extras in life. Parents who condone their child's every act and turn a blind eye to misbehavior do little beyond breeding a new generation of pride and folly. The person who must belittle his opponent to win an argument, who accepts praise but never blame, or who manipulates others to exalt himself, is ultimately on the losing end of a battle that has been fought throughout human history.

When pride sets in, we ignore our creaturely status and imagine ourselves as the Creator. Not in a literal sense, of course, but in a behavioral sense. We live as though we are masters of our destiny. We owe nothing to anyone and are entitled to all we desire. The ability to exalt ourselves by making others feel small gets easier along the way. Or maybe we don't overtly try to make others feel small, but we do nothing to make them feel differently. Status requires a pecking order. Pride requires those on the lower rungs to accept their place in the hierarchy. Pride absolves itself of most sins and rationalizes the rest. Pride inclines us to be haughty, boastful, vain, smug, self-righteous, hypocritical, condescending, demeaning, uncaring, short-tempered, and conceited. Did I leave anything out?

When the Bible condemns pride, that's the behavior it has in mind. The proud are offended by the claim God makes upon their lives. They are their own rulers. Hence, the claim God makes on them is offensive and resisted. Often it is not until such folks crash and burn that they come to see life differently. The adjustment is not easy.

The Bible warns:

> Pride comes before destruction, and an arrogant
> spirit before a fall. (Prov. 16:18)

Some pride is blatant. Napoleon's disastrous march on Moscow comes to mind. Adolph Hitler repeated that mistake during my childhood and got the same result. Such pride is evident not only in the world of nations but more commonly in the smaller world of our lives. A hungry man too proud to take a low-paying job, a woman who will sacrifice friendship over a minor slight, or the boss who demeans employees with a satisfaction that is both punitive and hypocritical. You and I can add a hundred more examples to the list. Many can be drawn straight from our own behavior.

Other forms of pride are subtle. Certain smiles can signal pride . . . as can scowling eyebrows . . . even silence when helpful words are needed. Humility itself can be a tool of pride, a mask for those who seek only to promote their virtue.

Pride is an over-the-top evaluation of ourselves and our opinions. At its core, pride is dishonest. It represents a refusal to evaluate ourselves in light of the relevant facts. In that regard, pride takes what is inherently good about us and turns it into something bad.

Odd, isn't it, that pride is not merely a rebellion against God but also a rebellion against our own true nature . . . an exercise in sadomasochism. The medical community regards neurosis as a form of mental distress. Neurosis involves paring down reality—or else reassembling it—in a manner that runs contrary to the facts. Various phobias—fear of flying, for instance—or obsessing over chocolate (my lifelong struggle!), are disorders in the sense that they incline us to dis-order reality by rearranging the facts in an unhealthy manner. In my case, after being diagnosed with Type 2 diabetes, I hid chocolate around the house so my wife wouldn't find it. Fortunately, she did, and my diabetes is under control. We all have neuroses to one degree or another. Some are innocuous—mere idiosyncrasies that make us unique and some-times the butt of our own jokes. Others are troubling and require the help of professionals. In the realm of spiritual experience, pride is the refusal to submit ourselves to ultimate truths about life. If those truths don't fit our game plan, we deny them in order to please ourselves. That's how the Scripture understands pride. The biblical writers experienced it themselves. They got smacked down by the Living God. Painfully so. Then they wrote about their experience—what they learned about themselves and life. Their confessions double as a warning.

Listen:

> You rescue an afflicted people, but Your eyes
> are set against the proud—You humble them.
> (2 Sam. 22:28)

> When pride comes, disgrace follows, but with
> humility comes wisdom. (Prov. 11:2)

> Pride comes before destruction, and an arrogant
> spirit before a fall. (Prov. 16:18)

> Human pride will be humbled, and the loftiness of
> men will be brought low; the LORD alone will be
> exalted on that day. (Isa. 2:11)

> I will bring disaster on the world, and their own
> iniquity, on the wicked. I will put an end to the
> pride of the arrogant and humiliate the insolence of
> tyrants. (Isa. 13:11)

Everyone with a proud heart is detestable to the
Lord; be assured, he will not go unpunished.
(Prov. 16:5)

Love is patient, love is kind. Love does not envy, is
not boastful, is not conceited. (1 Cor. 13:4)

All of these verses are rooted in personal experience. The biblical writers didn't sit around a campfire at night drinking alcohol and spinning aphorisms out of thin air. Nor were they cowards who sat on the sidelines of life resenting everyone else who had a better life than them. Rather, they were people who had been prideful in their own right and then got knocked down by the truth. And they repeated the error and got knocked down again. And again. Some kept getting knocked down until they were too bruised and broken to get up. Others learned more quickly. They all discovered the truth of what has been famously attributed to Albert Einstein:

Insanity is doing the same thing over and over again
and expecting different results.

Pride is a particular form of insanity that might best be defined as a lack of humility. Pride's footprints are recognizable no matter when they track through history. Yesterday? A generation ago? A millennia? The tracks all lead to the same cliff.

I am a big believer in the lessons of history. It was Harvard philosopher George Santayana who said a century ago:

Those who cannot remember the past are condemned to repeat it.

The cumulative testimony of history carries weight. We do well to hear its message. If everyone who visits the Grand Canyon comes away with a similar experience—namely, the experience of grandeur and majesty, along with a sense of one's own comparative smallness—I figure most others who look into that canyon in the future will tell a similar story. So it is with the experience of the Living God. Such encounters involve the misery of one's own prideful dishonesty and the liberating power of confession, surrender, and grace.

Now let me flip this entire conversation about pride upside-down. Every coin has two sides. Let's consider the underbelly of pride, the hidden motive. What is the cash value of being prideful, arrogant, haughty, and so forth? People don't succumb to pride for no reason at all. It's not like they wake up one morning and say to themselves, "I think I'll go out today and mess up the rest of my life for no good reason. Pride seems like a good way to do it. I can make myself miserable and others as well. A two-fer. That's the ticket!" We do well to dig a bit deeper than that.

What is it that inclines us to be prideful? It has much to do, I believe, with fear. A deep, dreadful fear. Private and threatening. It is the fear of acknowledging our own creatureliness. Such vulnerability is a threat we all understand. Fearing weakness, we pretend to be strong. Fearing wrong, we insist on being right. What we resent in ourselves, we despise in others. We are drawn to dishonesty and denial because they offer relief. They offer a shelter from the storm. Why be discomfited by acknowledging the truth about ourselves? It's much easier to live with lies. I doubt anyone ever thinks it out in those terms, but it seems to be the way the process works. As the need for dishonesty and denial increases, so does the threat of guilt and shame for choosing such a path. But the cost of admitting it is too dreadful to bear. So instead we double down on the lie. Such self-deception leaves us angry and resentful that we should have to feel this way at all. We want someone to blame. So we take aim at others. We demean them when they challenge us. We revile them for opposing us. We punish them for our own sins. After all, someone's blood must be spilled to make us feel better about ourselves. So others become our sacrificial lamb—our means of justification and salvation, if you will. We sacrifice them on the altar of our own unhappiness, aiming to give ourselves a worth that we cannot find any other way. "I shall lord it over you," the haughty say. But in their voice you hear the echo of a frightened child, alone and uncertain in a world of bad dreams. I do not say this to exonerate the arrogant and haughty. I mention it only to cite their weakness and shame. Pride is not a strength. It is a weakness borne of fear.

The Living God comes to satisfy our bloodlust. He tells us that the need for sacrifice already has been made. He made the sacrifice Himself, on our behalf, when He came in the flesh and dwelt among us.

> In the beginning was the Word, and the Word was
> with God, and the Word was God. He was with
> God in the beginning. All things were created
> through Him, and apart from Him not one thing
> was created that has been created. Life was in Him,
> and that life was the light of men. . . . The Word
> became flesh and took up residence among us. We
> observed His glory, the glory as the One and Only
> Son from the Father, full of grace and truth.
> (John 1:1–4, 14)

Out of love—and for reasons that faith allows only a glimmer of understanding—He chose to experience what we experience, in all of its depths. He bore the weight of creation. He experienced the fear and anxiety and anger that drive us toward pride. He saw how evil and wrathful pride can be. Proud people are deeply angry. They want someone to pay the price for their anger. *If it's blood you're after,* says the Living God, *put it on Me. I will bear the price of your anger. You will see the depth of My love and power. Then maybe you will fear Me alone and be healed.* Listen:

> He Himself bore our sins in His body on the tree,
> so that, having died to sins, we might live for right-
> eousness; you have been healed by His wounds.
> (1 Pet. 2:24)

He offered Himself. He did it purely out of love for His creation. So He tells us (my summary):

> Your fears were not My doing. Nor your anxieties.
> Yes, you have limitations. Yes, you have questions.
> But I have been here all along. And I have come to
> you more than once. I created you so we could have
> fellowship with one another. You have chosen oth-
> erwise. The sin of your pride lays squarely on you.
> You feel angry? You want someone to pay? So do I!
> I am grieved by your arrogance and stubbornness.
> And insulted that you would turn your back on
> Me. But I have made amends for all of us. My grief
> runs that deep. Look closely at the cross. Those are
> MY outstretched arms. That is MY blood. I am the
> embodiment of all those you chose to exalt yourself

above . . . the ones upon whom you focused your
scorn and sharpened your claws and trod underfoot. You, too, are among those I came to save.
I am the cost of your pride. I have satisfied the
demands of your sin. The price is paid. So let it go.
Let go of pride and all that goes with it. Leave the
fear and anxiety behind. It gets you nowhere but
lost. You're there already. Trust Me on this. Come
back home. Be the person I created you to be. I can
make you so. You are My child. I knitted you in the
womb. You are Mine.

Such is the love of the Living God. His love is strong enough
to oppose us, to set obstacles in our path and hardship in our
future, through a lifetime and to the end if need be. His love is
fierce and firm and sure. He knows the way we must go. And He
will do all He can to block us from dead-end journeys. But His
deepest yearning is to set us free. Indeed, He already has done
so. Blood we demand for our existence, and blood He gave. His
blood. Not that He had to, but that He chose to. Out of love. We
were not made for fear and anxiety. Pride was not our destiny.
We were made to enjoy Him and the creation He set around us.
Sometimes we must puff ourselves up in rebellion and fall to great
depths before we learn this lesson.

But pride is a difficult habit to break. As I said, it is rooted
deep in our emotions, down at the level of fear and dread. Telling
a prideful man he should be humble is about as useful as walking into a funeral home and telling everyone not to be sad. Mere
platitudes don't work. If they did, we could end war tomorrow by
telling everybody to love one another. *Voilà*, problem solved.

Yeah, right. My platitude might rest on centuries of tried and true experience, but the listener must discover it for himself, or else it remains a platitude. Fortunately, the Living God intervenes in our lives toward that very end. Humbling experiences come to us in one form or another. Usually we encounter them as a smackdown that leaves us groveling without defense. We all have stories to tell. Here's one of mine. It occurred early in my coaching career.

In 1957, at age twenty-seven, I was in my second year at South Georgia College. I loved my family, my job, and the challenge of building a winning football program. The job required long hours. When I got home at night, there was always a laundry list of chores to be done. I was lucky to have a devoted wife who loved her children. She also was willing to do whatever it took to make ends meet. Neither of us were afraid of hard work or long hours. Ann worked at the Sears Catalog store where people came to order various goods. Douglas, Georgia, was a small town. Maybe twelve thousand people. Sears couldn't afford to stock a store with all kinds of goods, so they opened an order house. From morning 'til night, her hours were as demanding as mine. I took on extra jobs to supplement our income. In the summertime I worked as a lifeguard at the college swimming pool, and after supper I walked down to Stubb's Tobacco Warehouse, where I worked the graveyard shift seven nights a week from 8:00 p.m. until 8:00 a.m. unloading and stacking bales of tobacco that came in from nearby farms. During the Christmas season, I got a job with the post office. I would put leather harness straps on my shoulders and lug a mail cart down Main Street to deliver and pick up packages for local businesses. Mind you, I was also the Athletic Director and Head Football Coach at the local college. My wife and I were too young to worry about status. And too hungry. We had mouths to feed. Bills had to be paid. Pride was too expensive. You do what you have to do. We both understood the ground rules. I was grateful for a wife who could outwork me any day of the week, and usually did.

That spring, the football player of my dreams showed up on campus. His teammates nicknamed him "Chief" because of his Cherokee Indian heritage. He looked every bit like a full-blooded Cherokee, with thick dark hair and a strong cut in his jaw. They meant the moniker as an honorary title of acceptance and camaraderie. Almost all the players were nicknamed by their teammates. Still, no one had designs on getting Chief upset. He stood six feet five and weighed over two hundred and fifty pounds. If he had body fat, it wasn't noticeable. In those days, an average defensive lineman might stand six feet tall and weigh two hundred pounds—an impressive size in 1957. Offensive linemen were about the same size. Chief dwarfed them all. He was a man among men. He was also as old as me, if not older, and claimed to have been a military veteran. I could only imagine the chaos he would create once we got him in a game. He had come to us after quitting the team at Florida State University. Rumor had it that he departed under circumstances that were less than favorable. I didn't know anybody in Tallahassee and didn't bother to ask. Players of his stature didn't come around often. I figured that as long as he played by the rules and didn't cause problems, his past didn't matter.

Oh, but it did.

Chief showed up for practice each day and worked as hard as every other player on the team. I admired the effort he gave. But it turned out that Chief had a true renegade's heart. Talk about not wanting to be confined in anyone's corral. The guy was a free spirit. He cut his own path in life. But not all the paths he cut were good ones. Alcohol was part of the problem. Those were days when many soldiers returned from war and attended college. They carried memories that few others understood. Alcohol often was part of their solution. Even if you didn't approve of drinking, you understood why they did.

One Saturday morning I got a call from the local sheriff. Chief had been arrested for drinking and fighting. After being put in a holding cell for intoxicated prisoners, he lit a mattress on fire and tried to burn the jail down—with him in it! The sheriff called that next morning as a favor to me. Long story short, we got Chief back on campus and I imposed a strict disciplinary regimen to help reform his bad judgment. I sat him down in the following days and explained that he should live as an example for others to follow. My speech ended with the admonition that if he chose to cause any more trouble, he'd better do it in some other county. I assumed he understood what I meant. I only wanted to emphasize the importance of being a good role model in the local community.

Well, so much for assumptions. Two weeks later I received a call from the sheriff of the adjoining county. Chief was in jail over in Ocilla, Georgia. This time it was a barroom brawl. He had given a pretty bad beating to some folks. It took seven deputies to get him under control. Once again I accepted him back on the team subject to further disciplinary measures.

I tried everything I knew to get Chief's life turned around, including counseling with him and taking him to church with my family. He tried hard to improve his behavior. He even showed his dedication at practice one day by announcing that I should hit him on the chin, right there in front of all the other players, as recompense for disobeying me! But try as he might, he simply couldn't reform himself. Other incidents occurred. One fight involved knives. Worries began to crop up about his mental stability. I wish I had been wise enough to help him, but I wasn't.

What I finally did was to visit him in his dorm room one day and tell a lie. I told him that the University of Southern Mississippi in Hattiesburg had a football scholarship for him, and that he should head that way immediately. Eager to play football at a big university, he packed his duffel bag and hitchhiked to Hattiesburg that very night, his thumb aiming toward the future.

Meanwhile, I advised the local sheriff not to allow him back into our county. Then I called the head coach at Southern Mississippi to tell him a big, brawny recruit had been sent his way. That's when I learned that Southern Miss was out of scholarships.

Two days later my home phone rang. We didn't have caller ID in those days. I answered. It was Chief. "Coach, you lied to me," he said. "They don't have a scholarship for me. What am I supposed to do?"

Chief really was talented enough to play for a major college team. I had good reason to think Southern Miss would give him a scholarship, assuming they had one. And they could provide better supervision. I had no staff members other than my assistant coach. We had no secretaries, no administrative helpers, nobody to help lighten the load. I was working outside jobs. And I had my hands full with a family of responsibilities at home. I felt fine about my conversation with Chief right up until the moment he called. Then truth smacked me down. Interesting, isn't it, how we rationalize things in our favor? That serpent from the Garden of Eden continues to exist because we continue to feed him. Ultimately we are his meal. It never seems that way at first.

Chief's call from Hattiesburg was humiliating. He probably had to borrow money just to make the call. What a shot to the heart. And rightfully so. And for him also, but in a different way. Life comes full circle for all of us. The proud are brought low. Liars eventually get their hands called. Whenever we pretend to be someone other than what God intended, we work against ourselves and become our own worst enemies. Being forced to learn humility is like having your face rubbed in the dirt. Such experiences can bring us to our knees. That's not a bad thing. Those who have been humbled learn the goodness of a simple and honest and dignified life. Pride is seen for what it is—a dishonesty that we commit upon ourselves. The Living God will bring us low if needed.

It's hard to believe I am telling a story that occurred almost sixty years ago. How could the time have passed so quickly?

As an afterthought, let me mention that Chief called me several years back. Apparently his life had turned in a new direction. All he could do was talk about Jesus and the difference faith made in his life. There was an energy and joy in his voice that swelled my heart. He called a few times afterward, even wrote me a letter from time to time. I rested easy knowing he had given over his life to his Creator. Our Creator. We both were young in those days, with much to learn. I haven't heard from him in the past two years. He may have made the final journey ahead of me. God be with him.

All good living is done on bended knee. When your knee is on the ground, your face is never far above the dirt from which you were made. That's a good starting point for any person who hungers for wisdom.

The most common word for *humility* in the Old Testament is *anah*. As I wrote earlier, the root meaning of most biblical words is drawn directly from experience. *Anah* is no exception. The word points to an image from real life . . . something we can visualize and immediately understand.

The Hebrew word *anah* means "bended knee." It evokes the image of someone kneeling reverently, in fear and trembling, in front of the conqueror. The bended knee is not an act of courtesy. The supplicant is not attempting merely to show deference to a superior. Or seek approval. Rather, the knee is bent in utter defeat. It is the final act of surrender. The vanquished kneels in submission to the victor's decision. If you are the person on bended knee, you are no longer thinking of yourself at all. Whatever pride and arrogance you had is shattered, strewn in pieces across the battlefield of your defeat. Status is irrelevant. Your life no longer is in your hands. All you can think of now is the victor and what the victor chooses.

The next time you come across the word *humility* in the Old Testament, know that some form of the word *anah* lies behind the English translation. It implies that some great strength has been exerted, some kind of body blow experienced, a defeat that drives one into the ground. And silence too. There is a silence involved, however momentary, when the loser awaits his fate and the victor has not yet announced it. The only certainty is the dirt beneath your knees . . . your head raised high enough only to see the feet of your conqueror. Whatever the verdict, you know your life will never be the same. Pride and arrogance have been crushed.

Anah.

"On bended knee."

Let that image sink in.

Curiously, when translators were looking for the English word that came closest in meaning to *anah*, they settled on the word *humility*. The word *humility* derives from the old Latin word *humus*, from which we get the idea of dirt or earthiness. The ancient Latins understood that life can drive us to the ground and smear our faces in the dirt . . . a vantage point that changes our view of ourselves. From *humus* comes *humility*. I suspect that every great culture in every age has a similar word, the root meaning of which is not much different from *anah* or *humus*. Life is what it is. The same God created us all. Our experiences cannot be all that different. Or the lessons we learn.

For the ancient Hebrews, the word *anah* captured their experience of the Living God. *Anah* is inevitable. The Living God chases us through our lifetimes. No one can escape Him. If *anah* doesn't happen now, it happens later. He sees to it because He loves us. He bears our sorrows but does not encourage sorrow. Indeed, He fights against it. And so He fights with us, against us, until finally we learn. Pride and arrogance are unacceptable. He created us to be better than that. And He will see that His will comes to pass.

Sometimes the bended knee is involuntary. In battle, the vanquished often fell on their knees hoping for mercy. On other occasions, the oppressed were wrongly forced onto bended knee by their oppressor. So in Exodus 1:11, when the Israelites in Egypt were forced into servitude, we are told that the Egyptians

> . . . assigned taskmasters over the Israelites to
> oppress [*anah*] them with forced labor.

And again, later in the Exodus story, the Living God confronts Pharaoh through the voice of Moses and says:

> "How long will you refuse to humble [*anah*] yourself before Me?" (Exod. 10:3)

This same *anah* was demanded of the Israelites by the Living God who delivered them from the *anah* of their Egyptian oppressors. He set it down as a commandment:

> Remember that the LORD your God led you on the entire journey these 40 years in the wilderness, so that He might humble you and test you to know what was in your heart, whether or not you would keep His commands. He humbled you by letting you go hungry; then He gave you manna to eat, which you and your fathers had not known, so that you might learn that man does not live on bread alone but on every word that comes from the mouth of the LORD. (Deut. 8:2–3)

The man who led them through the *anah* of their wilderness journey was none other than Moses, who encountered the Living God some years earlier in a burning bush. Who better to understand the new covenant with Yahweh . . . the ground rules of their new and saving relationship? We read:

> Moses was a very humble man, more so than any man on the face of the earth. (Num. 12:3)

It should come as no surprise that the best leaders are humble people. Not fearful. Not cowardly or insecure or lacking in confidence. Certainly not self-effacing. But not boastful or reckless either, or intent on setting themselves above others. There is a centeredness to them. A gentle balance. An unspoken dignity and a task to be accomplished. They are more certain than others about the next best step. Honesty guides them. It gives them clarity of vision. Their ears are always open to the voice of God. They live each day in reverent submission to someone much greater than themselves. Their egos are not stumbling blocks.

For those with an honest ear, here is a message from the Living God:

> [If] My people who are called by My name humble
> themselves, pray and seek My face, and turn from
> their evil ways, then I will hear from heaven, forgive
> their sin, and heal their land. (2 Chron. 7:14)

Here are the confessions of those who listened. Note the good fruit of their hard-won lessons:

> For You rescue an afflicted people, but You humble
> those with haughty eyes. (Ps. 18:27)

> For Yahweh takes pleasure in His people; He adorns
> the humble with salvation. (Ps. 149:4)

> The fear of the LORD is what wisdom teaches, and
> humility comes before honor. (Prov. 15:33)

And so Peter, the disciple of Jesus, said many years later:

> Clothe yourselves with humility toward one
> another, because God resists the proud but gives
> grace to the humble. (1 Pet. 5:5)

I am a sinner saved by grace. That is my confession and my mantra. When I doubt it, I repeat it until the waves of doubt recede. Otherwise, I will be required to learn it again from experience. The learning process is not pleasant.

Humility has nothing to do with highlighting our weaknesses or downplaying our strengths. We all do some things well and others poorly. There is nothing dishonorable in acknowledging the truth or accepting an honest compliment. What's the virtue of doing less? To think we must be self-effacing is to miss the point of humility. We should be grateful for our gifts and ashamed of our failings. There's no honor in being disingenuous. Deliberate self-effacement is just another form of pride. Experience of the Living God is what matters.

If some, convinced that humility is essential to wisdom, decide that tomorrow they will start deprecating themselves in public and disavowing all merit, I may applaud their intentions but I totally disagree with their understanding of humility. A humble man or woman is honest. Honesty requires humility. To acknowledge the truth about ourselves is to confess that we are creatures of spirit and clay, as prone to foible as to fame. Honest people will not sacrifice their dignity on the altar of public perception. Dignity is not the price of humility. Just the opposite. Humility gives us dignity. The honest and humble person does not bend a knee to anyone except the Living God. God's saving grace sets us free to live in truth. Pride and arrogance are a different matter. They must go. If we refuse, we will be driven again into the dirt beneath our knees. The Living God does not play games.

We often think the rich and famous are immune from the need to live humbly. Who among them is required to live on bended knee? Such quaint notions as *anah* or *humus* are for the hoi polloi—the commoners—those who barely have two nickels to rub together and who fantasize about wealth and power. The rich and famous can afford a different life, some suppose. They dance on the stage of life for million-dollar paydays and dwell on estates in private mansions, behind large walls with bodyguards and a vineyard in the backyard and a helicopter to whisk them to wherever. It's all glitz and glamour as best we can tell. That's the public perception, at least. But that's not reality. Yes, there are some who gloat and think themselves of a higher order. Some prefer to think of themselves as elite talents who reached for the brass ring and seized it on their own and feel entitled to live as they please with no regard for others. Some bask in the limelight and only want more. But not all of them. Or even most of them. That's my observation, at least. Fools exist on all ends of the spectrum. And with such foolishness comes the awful emptiness that strikes all who think themselves more than they are.

Do not doubt that the Living God crosses every person's doorstep. His message does not change. Nor do His demands. Nor does life itself, no matter how large our bank account or how finely tailored our clothes. God does not punish anyone for success. Success is like a vapor in the wind. And riches, though enjoyable, cannot buy what we yearn for the most. Errol Flynn was one of my early movie heroes. Then Gary Cooper and John Wayne. I loved the heroic roles they played—Flynn the dashing swashbuckler, Cooper the cold-eyed lawman or simple soldier, and John Wayne with his swaggering air of confidence. All three of those movie heroes have one thing in common—they are dead. The commonality is not insignificant. Fame and fortune had no bearing on their finitude. Or on the well-being of their families. Or on their happiness or sorrow. From dust we come and to dust we will return. Those who live with dust on their cheeks—who refuse to try and wipe it away in the name of pride and arrogance—are blessed with the gift of humility.

Humility allows us to live with dignity. Without humility, the default lifestyle is pride. Pride is a weakness, not a strength. It testifies to our insecurity and proneness to self-deception. It appears otherwise, I understand. How else can pride appear? Do you think a prideful person would ever reveal his soft spot or make himself vulnerable? Not a chance. The ego of the proud is tender. It requires protection. Arrogance is a defensive response. Skunks ward off attackers with a potent spray. Wishing to be other than they know themselves to be, they embrace adulation, sometimes blushing as a means to encourage even more. The beast must be fed. Such folks can become callous and cruel, especially when they believe their own lies. They thrive on flattery and a pledge of fealty. Woe to anyone who fails to deliver. The ego of the proud is not strong enough to allow a challenge. They wrestle with demons you never see. And they will crush you under foot if you threaten them. Dignity is not their strong suit. Dignity belongs only to the humble. Only the dignified can hold their heads high no matter what.

In humility we rise from the ashes of self-deceit and discover our true worth. Such worth is honestly bestowed and honestly kept. We have had this worth since the day our Creator fashioned us from the earth. Yes, indeed, we have dirt on our knees. What else can one expect from people fashioned from the soil? But God had a plan. And a blessing ordained from the beginning of time. Listen to the word of our Creator. This is His pronouncement immediately after our creation:

> God saw all that He had made, and it was very
> good. (Gen. 1:31)

You are good. Eternally good. So am I. We have been blessed since the beginning of time. What a shame if we squander our inheritance. We find our goodness only in relationship with our Creator. If we strive for something different, disappointment beckons. Goodness goes unfound.

We live in a sinful world. Pride is the coin of the realm. The wise know better than to trade in that currency.

We are sinners saved by grace. With such an experience comes a lifestyle.

The Living God invites us to discover it.

CHAPTER 6

THE WISDOM
of PATIENCE

By your endurance you will gain your souls.
(Luke 21:19)

P atience is the art of waiting well. Blessed are those who can do so.

I heard a story many years ago. Three women all happened to arrive at the pearly gates at the same time. St. Peter, the gatekeeper, greeted them and kindly asked if they would please wait a bit, as he had some pressing matters that needed his attention. He was gone a long while. Upon his return, he went to one of the women, apologized for the lengthy delay, and asked if she minded the wait.

Not at all, she replied. *I have waited a lifetime to be in heaven. Just standing by the gate is a thrill.*

That's wonderful, said Peter. *I have but one question to ask. How do you spell "God?"*

G-O-D, she replied.

Excellent, said Peter. *Please come in.*

He approached the second woman, made the same apology and asked if she had minded the wait.

Oh, no. It was no trouble at all. I want so much to see everyone inside.

One more thing, said Peter. *How do you spell "God?"*

Why, it's G-O-D, she said.

Perfect, he replied. She, too, was admitted into heaven.

He then went to the third woman and asked if she had minded the wait.

Ha! she said in a huff. *This is typical of every place I've been. All they do is make you wait. I had to wait in line to vote, wait in line at the movies, wait in line at the grocery store. Now I get here and what's the first thing that happens? More waiting!*

Well, I'm sorry for your many inconveniences, said Peter. *But the Lord is merciful and gracious. Such things can be put behind us now. There is, however, one other question I want to ask.*

What is it? she said with an impatient roll of her eyes.

St. Peter returned her look and asked, *How do you spell "Czechoslovakia?"*

We all know what it is to wait. No one particularly enjoys it. Yet we spend much of our lives doing it. We wait in line. We wait for a call. We wait in traffic. We wait for others. *C'mon, get a move on,* we sometimes quietly mutter, *I haven't got all day.* And indeed we don't, if you think in terms of a single lifetime.

Considering how few days we have on earth—where the clock is always ticking—it is amazing how much time we actually do spend waiting.

Waiting is such a common experience that some people make a career of it. They *wait on people* for a living. You'll find them working at your local restaurant. Others dedicate office space to it. *Have a seat in the Waiting Room,* the receptionist tells us, *the doctor will see you shortly.* The word *shortly,* I have come to suspect, is the medical term for *extended waiting.* Not even language is immune. We all are familiar with catch-phrases such as . . . *Wait a minute . . . Wait and see . . . Wait for me. . . Wait right there . . . Wait it out . . . Wait your turn . . . Wait 'til next year.*

Simply put, waiting is inescapable. No one can avoid having to do it. You would think after a few years of practice we all would be good at waiting. Yet just the opposite proves true. Waiting often causes frazzled nerves, irritability, high blood pressure, unkind words, road rage and sometimes even depression and despair. Toes tap and fingers strum as we fill the empty moments of some unnecessary delay or another, often accompanied with a tedious sigh. We all know people who get irritated by the slightest inconvenience. They vent their spleen, making sure everyone around them gets an earful. They gripe and grumble and look for someone to blame. And woe unto those who become the targets of their frustration. I suspect every employee who has spent much time *waiting* on customers can recall a half-dozen such malcontents in the blink of an eye. Kudos to those who manage to wait out another person's tirade without blowing a gasket themselves. Little acts of grace occur all around us every day. Sometimes grace comes in the form of waiting out those who have no grasp of waiting well.

The quality of one's physical health should be reason enough for anyone to yearn for patience. Anger is such a destructive emotion. Like the detonation of a nuclear bomb, the blast itself passes rather quickly but the damage is long-lasting. Who wouldn't want to master the art of waiting well if only to live more peacefully?

So averse are we to waiting that we measure a person's worth by how little waiting he or she has to do. Have you ever been taken to the front of the line ahead of everyone else? Special feeling, isn't it? A sign of status. You almost feel guilty that you don't have to *wait* like everyone else. *Save my place in line,* we tell our friends at other times. And where exactly is *my place* except in relation to those unfortunate souls who are less well-placed. Of those who don't have to wait, we think, *Man, they have it made.* Few phrases are as disheartening as *You'll have to go to the back of the line.* Having to wait when we would prefer otherwise is a reminder of our relative insignificance in the grander scheme of things. It's another way of being reminded we are not so important as we think.

Our particular age is one of deep anger and impatience. Of course, a stagnant economy, mounting debt and high unemployment put a lot of people on edge. I think of struggling business owners who teeter on the brink of bankruptcy, for whom *wait 'til next year* has become the annual mission statement, or the anxious parent who smiles during each job interview knowing her creditors won't wait much longer. A lot of people are angry in today's world. What does God mean when he asks them to live patiently? How can one *wait well* when the business may be shuttered or the bills go unpaid? I believe that patience is not merely helpful but also essential in such circumstances. The key is to understand what Scripture means by patience. But let me not get ahead of myself just now.

Technology—particularly digital technology—also plays a major role in the impatience of modern life. Science and industry have provided us with many time-saving conveniences. They cut our waiting times on everything from food to phone calls. Not that I am complaining at all about progress. I'm not above a fast-food sandwich when I'm hungry and in a hurry. And the microwave is my friend. I use it often, sometimes right after I press the button that brews my coffee in less than a minute! When I was a child, ground coffee was put in a pot of hot water and allowed to steep. Then came percolators, which could brew coffee in a mere twenty minutes or so. Then Mr. Coffee showed up and cut the waiting time to a fraction of that. More recently, advances in digital technology have cut our waiting time for many other activities in life. I own a laptop, a smart phone and a tablet. My work requires them. In an instant I can cast a vote in the latest football poll, respond to an inquiry, or participate in a video interview. Airport delays are not the drudgery they once were. At least I can answer e-mails, watch YouTube videos or get caught up on topics of interest while I wait out the delay. Digital technology is immediate gratification on steroids.

As we become more accustomed to immediate gratification, other traditional factors play into our modern age of impatience. Laziness is one of them. Who wants to endure delays or pay the price of endurance if quitting is easier? A slothful person, for instance, needs exercise and a good diet. It's a matter of personal wellbeing. Discipline is needed. But discipline requires sustained effort. One must eat right and exercise on a regular basis. Yuk. What fun is that? And who has time? It is much easier to invent excuses for the person we see in the mirror.

Selfishness plays the biggest role, however, and on a number of levels. Impatience ultimately is an ego issue. Like the person who says, *I want patience and I want it now,* we like things to be done our way and on our schedule. Those who work at a different pace or otherwise impose upon our schedules are a burden. Employers who hire someone for a job have every right to expect that person to complete tasks in a timely manner. But no two people are the same. Few people share an identical vision for life. A wise employer takes these variations into account and works to help employees become more productive. A fool simply shouts out orders and expects everyone to conform. The same principle applies in family life and in the public marketplace. Patience is the variable. As long as we put ourselves at the center of the universe, long-term frustration and disappointment are bound to result.

Yet despite the rising tide of impatience in modern life, some people have mastered the art of waiting well. They exhibit a serenity that is difficult to describe. They are more compassionate than most. Gentle and understanding. Forgiving. We wish we could wait like they do. Their eyes seem to peer beyond the waiting moment, focused on something in the distance that patience will help them acquire. Their pace is different from ours. And steadier. More assured. What is it that they see? That they aim for? They live as though no waiting moment is wasted. Their hidden strength . . . their vision . . . their centeredness and sense of purpose is what we admire. We want to emulate them.

It may surprise some to learn that Scripture makes a big deal about patience. The topic is raised time and again. Biblical writers claim that peace, happiness, mental clarity, good judgment, serenity, and personal fulfillment are the fruits of patience. Listen:

A patient person shows great understanding,
but a quick-tempered one promotes foolishness.
(Prov. 14:29)

A hot-tempered man stirs up conflict, but a man
slow to anger calms strife. (Prov. 15:18)

Patience is better than power, and controlling one's
temper, than capturing a city. (Prov. 16:32)

The end of a matter is better than its beginning; a
patient spirit is better than a proud spirit. Don't let
your spirit rush to be angry, for anger abides in the
heart of fools. (Eccl. 7:8–9)

A ruler can be persuaded through patience, and a
gentle tongue can break a bone. (Prov. 25:15)

So we must not get tired of doing good, for we
will reap at the proper time if we don't give up.
(Gal. 6:9)

Therefore, God's chosen one, holy and loved, put on
heartfelt compassion, kindness, humility, gentleness,
and patience, accepting one another and forgiving one another if anyone has a complaint against
another. Just as the Lord has forgiven you, so you
must also forgive. (Col. 3:12–13)

So that you won't become lazy but will be imitators
of those who inherit the promises through faith and
perseverance. (Heb. 6:12)

And we exhort you, brothers: warn those who are irresponsible, comfort the discouraged, help the weak, be patient with everyone. (1 Thess. 5:14)

We begin to understand these biblical references when we ponder those experiences in life when patience clearly pays a rich dividend. Think about waiting on those we love. A mother waits quietly as her daughter sounds out each word in a storybook. She offers instruction but resists the temptation to interrupt more than necessary. The daughter's smile of achievement is what she's after. Standing in front of the mirror, a father teaches his son the proper way to knot a tie. The procedure is something the father performs every morning with ease as he dresses for work. His young son can't seem to get the over and under of it. At stake is the boy's aim to become a man. The father helps guide his son through the loops, maybe a half dozen times or more, until the boy gets it right. In these instances, and in so many others, waiting is desirable. We do it because we care. Our satisfaction is found in the result it brings. Patience becomes an act of sacrificial love and self-fulfillment.

Other times we wait because we aim to achieve an ideal, one out in the far distance but well worth the wait. Anyone who aspires to noble character, for instance, must learn the virtue of patience. Good character does not come ready-made. Experience is required. Time must pass. One's commitments must be tried and tested more than once. Like an aspiring marathon runner, one cannot expect to develop endurance in a mere week or two. Some long-term goals are worth the patience needed to achieve them. Creating a good marriage and raising children are further examples. So, too, is building a career and cultivating friendships.

Each good step takes one closer to the goal. Satisfaction grows, though not without occasional setbacks. Time is the prerequisite. Such waiting takes energy and commitment.

Some people equate waiting with idle time. Waiting, in such a view, is merely the ability to endure some unnecessary delay without blowing one's stack—a kind of grin-and-bear-it view. Actually, that is more a formula for high-blood pressure and an early heart attack. Knowing how to wait well means something quite different.

Words that the Bible associates with patience—*endurance, perseverance, steadfastness and fortitude*—are action words. They indicate a person's determined engagement with obstacles that take effort to overcome. Anyone who has attempted a marathon knows that endurance requires a willingness to work through pain. One starts out running a mile or two without quitting. Sometime later, the length is stretched to four miles, then ten, then fifteen. Along the way your legs ache. You heave for breath. You want to quit. But you don't. No one would ever complete their training for a marathon if pain meant it was time to quit. One must fight through the pain . . . experience it and bear it and build the strength to overcome it. I wish there was an easier way, but in many circumstances of life there is not. Eventually, the pain diminishes and endurance grows. One gets stronger in the process. *No pain, no gain* is an oft-repeated adage in sports. You push yourself from *can to can't,* and when you get to your limit you push yourself a little harder. Perseverance. Endurance. Fortitude. We coaches didn't invent those terms. We learned them the same place everyone learns them—from daily experience in the real world. Football just happens to be a venue where the virtue is essential to success. Players want to play their best. Coaches want to coach their best. There are no shortcuts around perseverance, endurance, and fortitude. In the realm of sports cliches, you've got to *keep your eyes on the prize.* In the spiritual realm where life really matters, the operative phrase is *faith in the Living God.* Lose that vision and you never reach the goal.

This virtue is especially needed when we suffer loss. Life is not fair. Some things we treasure dearly may be taken from us and never given back. A deeper form of patience is needed. I think of soldiers who return from combat missing legs that once carried them across the finish line or arms that once held a loved one. Artificial limbs will not replace the sense of touch that is missing or the range of experience once enjoyed. I think of parents who lose a precious child or those afflicted with maladies or caught in the snare of some awful calamity. *What is my future now?* they ask. *What is the point of waiting for something I will never get back?* The sufferer's loss is not an abstraction. It is palpable. Deeply personal. Real and threatening.

Waiting well in such moments requires one to endure despair. Despair can happen to anyone. Enduring it successfully is the achievement. Time is required. One goes to sleep in grief and wakes to more of the same. Sometimes for days on end. Daily life in such moments can become little more than a reflex action, done without thought or emotion and for no particular reason. It is a middle passage. For a while, the waiting seems pointless. One isn't sure how a next step is to be made at all.

After the destruction of Jerusalem in 586 BC, the survivors were hauled off to Babylon in captivity. They were forced to walk all the way. Gone were their homes and communities. Gone was the Temple where they worshipped. Gone were familiar voices and the mountains they knew so well. The dust of a long journey filled their throats. Fire and smoke were their last memories of Jerusalem. Bondage was the new reality. The Psalmist tells us what happened next:

> By the rivers of Babylon—there we sat down and wept when we remembered Zion. There we hung up our lyres on the popular trees, for our captors there asked us for songs, and our tormentors, for rejoicing: "Sing us one of the songs of Zion." How can we sing the LORD's song on foreign soil? (Ps. 137:1–4)

Indeed, how to sing the Lord's song in a foreign land. That's what suffering and loss come to in the end, isn't it?

How one chooses to make peace with loss determines the kind of *waiting* we will do. For many, the decision is a lonely one.

In such desolate moments, it is not uncommon to hear the words of those who have gone before and wonder what they meant. What did they discover that buoyed their spirits and restored their hope? Listen:

> I sought the LORD, and He answered me and delivered me from all my fears. (Ps. 34:4)

> For you delivered me from death, even my feet from stumbling, to walk before God in the light of life. (Ps. 56:13)

> For he will rescue the poor who cry out and the afflicted who have no helper. (Ps. 72:12)

In many ways, working through pain and despair is similar to breaking the stranglehold of a serious chemical dependency. The addict not only needs the patience of others, but he also must be patient with the recovery process. Recovery doesn't happen overnight. It takes time. That's why *perseverance* is needed. Both body and mind must adjust to the change. That's why *endurance* is needed. Temptations will arise. That's why *steadfastness* is needed. The desire to quit will rise time and again. That's why *fortitude* is needed.

We can draw deep inspiration from those—both present and past—who have suffered like us but by grace endured and persevered and were lifted out of despair. The author of Hebrews took this view when he wrote:

> Therefore, since we also have such a large cloud
> of witnesses surrounding us, let us lay aside every
> weight and the sin that so easily ensnares us. Let
> us run with endurance the race that lies before us,
> keeping our eyes on Jesus, the source and perfecter
> of our faith, who for the joy that lay before Him
> endured a cross and despised the shame and has sat
> down at the right had of God's throne. For con-
> sider Him who endured such hostility from sinners
> against Himself, so that you won't grow weary and
> lose heart. (Heb 12:1–3)

In the light of that conviction and his own personal experience, Paul wrote these words of encouragement to believers in the small town of Colossae:

May you be strengthened with all power, according to His glorious might, for all endurance and patience, with joy giving thanks to the Father, who has enabled you to share in the saints' inheritance in light. (Col 1:11–12)

When you stop to consider it, Paul's statement seems a bit odd. We tend to think of patience as a stoic virtue—the ability to suffer inconvenience and tolerate what is otherwise a waste of our time. In this view, *waiting well* is just a way of passing time until the inconvenience passes. But Paul speaks of patience quite differently. He equates patience with strength and power. Those sound like fighting words to me. And they are. There's nothing idle or passive about patience. Patience is dynamic. Active. When you stake your life on a vision, you push through setbacks. You grapple with obstacles. You refuse to give in. At times when you are too weak and wounded to get up off the floor, you raise your eyes and stare through your adversary toward the goal that lies beyond. And when the suffering is so intense that you no longer have strength to resist, you reach over and grab the hand of someone who does have strength and hold onto them until your own strength returns. Patience is how one embraces an adversary with the goal of conquering it. Sounds a lot like salvation, doesn't it?

That's precisely how Jesus understood it. He saw that patience and salvation are inseparable. Had they not been, he would have cut and run long before his final trip to Jerusalem. He did not speak to his disciples as a speculative theologian. There were no Ivy League schools in his day. No Oxford or Cambridge. He didn't own a Ph.D. And he possessed no special powers that were not available to anyone else who dared to trust the Living God.

He wrestled with the same uncertainties and liabilities that plague us. He shared our pathos as well as our joys. Such was the sheer mystery of his divine yet human existence, as John understood it:

> In the beginning was the Word, and the Word was with God, and the Word was God. . . . The Word became flesh and took up residence among us. We observed His glory, the glory as the One and Only Son from the Father. (John 1:1, 14)

By that John meant that God took on all the frailties of human existence. Blood, sweat and tears were experiences he embraced. The only difference is that Jesus did not lose sight of the vision. He looked beyond the adversary. He dared to believe to the end. It wasn't easy, but he did. During his life, and through his death and resurrection, he revealed the truth to all who would listen. Therein lies the grace and glory that God offers us through his Son, the *Word made flesh*. God shows us what he intended for us to know all along. To do so, he became like us. He shared our frailty. He spoke from inside his own all-too-human experience. *You want to know what it is like to persevere even when you are sweating bullets and aren't sure of the outcome,* he said. *Listen and I'll tell you. Even better, watch!* He showed us what can happen if we keep our eyes on the goal.

Mark's Gospel tells us that when Jesus was dying on the cross, his strength finally broke and he cried out in desperation:

> My God, by God, why have You forsaken me?
> (Matt. 27:46)

What a desperate and lonely moment that must have been, as he felt his life slipping away. Yet should we be surprised that Jesus was not spared from such a dark experience? Should we be surprised that he felt alone and abandoned by God in his darkest hour of need? The author of Hebrews reminds us:

> For we do not have a high priest who is unable to sympathize with our weaknesses, but One who has been tested in every way as we are,t yet without sin. (Heb. 4:15)

Feeling godforsaken is not a sin. Forsaking God is. There's a difference. Jesus went to the cross daring to wait on God. What is trust if not waiting? Waiting for someone we depend on. Waiting with our life on the line. That's what Jesus did.

Paul expressed it differently when he wrote to the church at Philippi, saying:

> If then there is any encouragement in Christ, if any consolation of love,a if any fellowship with the Spirit, if any affection and mercy, fulfill my joy by thinking the same way,d having the same love,e sharing the same feelings, focusing on one goal. Do nothing out of rivalry or conceit, but in humility consider others as more important than yourselves. Everyone should look out not only for his own interests, but also for the interests of others. Make your own attitude that of Christ Jesus, who, existing in the form of God, did not consider equality with God as something to be used for His own advantage. Instead He emptied Himself by assuming the

form of a slave, taking on the likeness of men. And
when He had come as a man in His external form,
He humbled Himself by becoming obedient to
the point of death—even to death on a cross. (Phil.
2:1–8)

Patience is at heart a religious issue. It is a gift that comes only
from God. Salvation and patience are inseparable. Thus Jesus told
his disciples in the days before Jerusalem:

By your endurance gain your lives. (Luke 21:19)

He is saying that if you are patient and don't give up, you
will find what you are looking for. What you seek is yourself, the
life you sense you were created to enjoy. Along the way, you will
encounter afflictions, reproaches, indignities and persecutions.
Stay on the path. Sacrifice will be demanded. Don't allow yourself
to be driven aside. Endure and you will have what you long for.

This fits with what Jesus said to his disciples on another occasion when he remarked:

For whosoever wants to save his life will lose it, but
whosoever loses his life because of Me and the gospel will save it. (Mark 8:35)

Patience requires letting go. What we let go of are the irrita-
tions, frustrations, anger and despair of our old lives. Our eyes
once were set on ourselves. On the immediate gratification of
our desire. We might defer gratification for a short while, if the
gain was great enough, but waiting had limits. Pain and suffering threatened that old life. Death marked its end. Impatience set

in because we were determined to experience the good fruit of life on our terms as often and as quickly as we could. Anything that delayed our satisfaction evoked an impatient reaction. Now our eyes are set on a new goal. The obstacles are still there. They didn't magically disappear. The faithful are still subject to sickness and suffering. The loss of worldly assets or precious family members can happen to us as easily as to anyone. But our view of loss changes—or rather, can change—as we give ourselves to God daily and let him complete his good work in us. For those who learn to wait well, God's will becomes their desire. It's a lesson in faith that takes time to learn. Good habits are not created overnight. It requires a process of dying to self and living for God. Our old selves would not have been willing to pay that price. But in Christ we die to the old impatient self and are filled with the strength to remain steadfast and endure. All good things in life come to us as a gift through the grace of God. Patience is one of those gifts. The more we put our lives in God's hands, the more we take on his personality. And patience is one of God's defining characteristics.

> But you, Lord, are a compassionate and gracious
> God, slow to anger and rich in faithful love and
> truth. (Ps. 86:15)

> Yet He was compassionate: He atoned for their
> guilt and did not destroy them. He often turned
> His anger aside and did not destroy them. He often
> turned His anger aside and did not unleash all His
> wrath. (Ps. 78:38)

God, within Your temple, we contemplate Your
faithful love. (Ps. 48:9)

The Lord does not delay His promise, as some
understand delay, but is patient with you, not
wanting any to perish but all to come to repentance.
(2 Pet. 3:9)

Or do you despise the riches of His kindness,
restraint, and patience, not recognizing that God's
kindness is intended to lead you to repentance?
(Rom. 2:4)

Not all of our desires will be fulfilled in this lifetime. Whether
one accepts or rejects faith—or chooses to live impatiently rather
than patiently—that fact will not change. The life God fills us
with now will be brought to completion in God's time, not in
ours. This side of death we are given a foretaste. What we are
allowed to taste is the very nature and spirit of the Living God.

A local pastor attended one of my football practices back at
South Georgia in the 1950s. He stood on the sideline during one
of those hot, sweltering mornings in August when the breeze
disappears and the temperature is almost unbearable. It wasn't
uncommon for a player's tongue to stick to the roof of his mouth
during practice because so much body fluid was sweated out. The
heat took its toll on the coaches, too. After practice that day, we
left the field, cleaned up, and headed to the dining hall for lunch.
The first order of business was to fill our bodies with all the liquid
we could consume. The pastor stuck around to join me at lunch.
On this particular occasion, as I was sliding my tray down the
cafeteria line ahead of the minister, I came to a big vat of ice-cold

orange drink. You could see the crushed ice floating around inside. Beads of condensation dripped down the outside of the vat. The mere sight of it is still vivid in my memory. I grabbed a plastic glass, filled and drank it on the spot, then re-filled it and drank again. Nearly sixty years later, I remember how good it felt to get that liquid in my body. That's when the minister saw a teachable moment and said to me: *Bobby, God is like that big vat of orange drink. You could never consume it all. But you don't have to drink the whole thing to know how good it tastes.*

God dwells among us and reaches out to us every day, but his base of operations is in a different time zone from ours. His clock does not mark time the same way our clocks do. The Psalmist said of the Living God:

> For in Your sight a thousand years are like
> yesterday that passes by, like a few hours of the
> night. (Ps. 90:4)

Waiting well requires us to wait for God and trust His timing. To put it differently, waiting well means to remind ourselves time and again—especially when troubles mount up—that God is in control. Such waiting gives us confidence. We gain strength. Our endurance grows. Hope burns brighter. And those encumbrances that once dragged us down slowly lose their grip.

> But those who trust in the LORD will renew their
> strength; they will soar on wings like eagles; they
> will run and not grow weary; they will walk and not
> faint. (Isa. 40:31)

Such is the wisdom of faith. To know life in its fullness, I must wait on God just as Jesus did. I wish I could climb into the heavens and view time from God's perspective. Life would make more sense. It certainly would help me do a better job of waiting. But no ladder reaches that high. The folks in Babel tried it many years ago. They built a tower. It didn't work. It never works. So I must trust and wait. Such waiting helps me look beyond the inconveniences and delays in daily life that can so easily cause frustration and irritation. Those delays are not so much an inconvenience as they are a challenge. They test my ability to look beyond them . . . my ability to get off my clock and on God's clock. It requires me to think of life from the standpoint of eternity. When I do, the inconveniences become an opportunity to prove the truth of the Living God.

Such was the apostle Paul's experience. He sacrificed far more than I ever have been asked to give. Yet he counted those losses as insignificant. How could he have patiently endured such sacrifice? The answer is simple yet profound. He had learned to look beyond such moments, his eyes fixed on something in the distance. I'll let him explain:

> But everything that was a gain to me, I have considered to be a loss because of Christ. More than that, I also consider everything to be a loss in view of the surpassing value of knowing Christ Jesus my Lord. Because of Him I have suffered the loss of all things and consider them filth, so that I may gain Christ and be found in Him, not having a righteousness of my own from the law, but one that is through faith in Christs—the righteousness from God based on faith. My goal is to know Him and the power of His

resurrection and the fellowship of His sufferings,u
being conformed to His death, assuming that I will
somehow reach the resurrection from among the
dead. Not that I have already reached the goal or am
already fully mature, but I make every effort to take
hold of it because I also have been taken hold of by
Christ Jesus. Brothers, I do not consider myself to
have taken hold of it. But one thing I do: Forget-
ting what is behind and reaching forward to what
is ahead, I pursue as my goal the prize promised by
God's heavenly call in Christ Jesus. (Phil. 3:7–14)

Reading this passage often reminds me of an exchange of
letters between my mother and me in 1966. October 1 was her
birthday. The date fell right in the middle of football season. I
was an assistant coach at West Virginia University in that year. It
wasn't until I got to the office that morning that I realized it was
her birthday. I immediately called a florist in Birmingham and
had a dozen roses sent. Later that day, when I had a free moment,
I wrote her a letter. We wrote letters in those days rather than
made phone calls. Handwritten letters seemed more personal. I
again wished her a happy birthday, told her what a wonderful
mother and person she was, closed it with *Love, Bobby,* and then
added:

PS: *I hope you live to be a hundred.*

One week later I received a reply by mail. She thanked me for
the roses and for the Happy Birthday letter. Then, in her deft and
gentle manner, she ended her letter with this:

PS: *Thank you for wishing that I might live to be one hundred. But don't worry about it. When I was a teenager, I turned my life over to Christ as my Savior. He guaranteed that I will live forever.*

So she wrote. And so she lived. And so she died. I have spent a lifetime inspired by the standard that she and my father established for me.

I mention this story not because I am maudlin or wish to brag on my mother. I share it only because she showed what a powerful influence mothers can be. I know it because I experienced it. Every young mother today has that same power to influence her children. Mothers are one of God's greatest tools. A good mother can mold the future for generations to come. So can a good father. Or a good friend. Patience is one of the greatest lessons my mother taught me, not so much by word as by deed. She had the power of her convictions.

I now have lived more than eight decades. *Life is a vapor,* the Psalmist wrote. And it is. At age five, a fifth of my lifetime was spent waiting for my sixth birthday. I remember being five-and-a-half. Such fractions made the wait a bit more tolerable at that age. Now I wait less than an eightieth of my lifetime for the same annual event. Time blows by faster than we realize. At age eighty you start buying Chapstick by the box.

In retrospect, I see more clearly that patience has little to do with tolerating life's inconveniences and everything to do with the person one wants to become. Waiting well is a power. Through patience God molds us into the persons he wanted us to be all along. The result is something that no one can take from us.

Listen again to the apostle Paul:

But the fruit of the Spirit is love, joy, peace,
patience, kindness, goodness, faith, gentleness,
self-control. Against such things there is no law.
(Gal. 5:22–23)

Did you catch what he says in that last sentence? Better yet, have you experienced it? *There is no law against such things,* he says. In other words, there is no power that can deprive you of the strength that comes from the Living God. No one can keep you from enjoying these fruits of the Spirit. And no one can take them from you. No person. No government. No threat. No obstacle.

And so we wait for God to complete the work He has begun in us. In his strength, we learn to wait well.

Such is the wisdom of patience.

CHAPTER 7

THE WISDOM
of DISCIPLINE

No discipline seems enjoyable at the time, but painful.
Later on, however, it yields the fruit of peace and
righteousness to those who have been trained by it.
(Heb. 12:11)

I didn't want the whipping I was about to get.

"Lean over the bed," my father said. His voice was terse. Resistance would only make matters worse. I glanced around and saw the belt slip through the loops around his waist. It was the narrow brown belt he wore to work. I wish it had been a different one. Narrow belts stung. Fortunately for me, he doubled it over to make it more like a strap than a whip—a kindness that others might not recognize. Yet his eyes bored through me. I searched them a second longer. They lacked the mercy I longed for. Hope slipped away. My knees leaned into the edge of the bed in partial submission to his command. Neither of us spoke further. What could I say in self-defense? He had warned me, not once but several times. I had a penchant for bad decisions. Not destructive decisions, mind you. I didn't start house fires or bully smaller kids in the neighborhood. I was a typical boy of my generation who got into typical mischief—only, on this occasion, what I did was over the top. It didn't seem so at the time. But it put me on the business end of his brown leather belt. This was going to hurt.

Let me explain. The trouble started on Christmas morning in 1940, when I was eleven. My father knew I wanted a BB gun for Christmas. All the kids had one. I mentioned the subject frequently as the holidays approached. My father showed little interest. But lo and behold, on Christmas morning, what did I find beneath the tree? A double-barrel BB gun! I had never seen one like it. In fact, I might have been the only kid in the neighborhood to have the double-barrel version. He couldn't have given me a better gift. No doubt my buddies would be jealous.

"You better not shoot anybody," he sternly admonished. I was aiming the BB gun around the house when he gave me the warning, and he repeated it again for emphasis. I wasn't listening. I was too busy gazing out the window in search of Nazi storm troopers. There hadn't been any reports of a Third Reich presence in Birmingham, Alabama, but I kept vigilant watch anyway, at least until my mother served breakfast.

After breakfast, I decided that I needed to go hunting. We lived in a neighborhood of small brick houses. A long row of oaks shaded the sidewalk out front beside the street. In those days every street had a sidewalk on either side, given that most people walked to places like church or the grocery or the doctor's office, all of which were within a few blocks. If I was going to have any luck hunting, I would need to walk down to the college campus. The campus was shrouded beneath huge oak trees. I planned on finding some squirrels, maybe enough to fill a pot for Brunswick stew. Or else some pigeons. Pigeons were always hanging out on window ledges and along rooftops at the college. One way or another I aimed to bag some critters. So off I went down the sidewalk, full of purpose. The only thing I lacked was a fur-skin Daniel Boone cap.

I reached the campus and meandered through a copse of oak trees just beyond the south end of the football field. My eyes searched the limbs for any signs of motion. As I crept beneath the trees, the football field came into view. Several boys were hanging around at the far end. No telling what they were up to. I studied them for a few minutes. My hunting instincts had kicked in at that point, and I wanted to test my BB gun on a moving target. I crouched behind a tree and kept my eyes on them. They seemed to be loitering. One of them looked familiar. I recognized him. It was Jack Spivey, a classmate and friend, standing with two other boys that I didn't know. Jack was a nice guy. I figured he wouldn't mind. So I took aim at his feet. He was at least a hundred yards away. My finger slipped down and notched onto the trigger. Ignorant of such factors as windage and distance, I took dead aim at his sneakers. Why I did so, I don't know. But I did. The trigger gave way to the curl of my finger. *Pfft.* The shot was off. I saw a commotion among Jack and his friends. Jack hopped around like he had been stung by a wasp. Apparently, a BB shot from a double-barrel BB gun carried farther than I imagined. No one appeared hurt, so I figured it might be best if I eased on out of there.

As I ambled up the sidewalk toward my house a while later, I noticed some folks on the front porch. It was Jack Spivey and his father. Jack's father was talking to my father. They all turned to look at me as I walked up. The double-barrel BB gun was slung over my shoulder. In retrospect, I should've ditched it. Anyway, that's how I came to be leaning over the bed on Christmas Day. "You better not shoot anybody," my father had told me that morning as I headed out the door. "I didn't think I could hit him from that far away," I explained to him and Mr. Spivey. And I didn't. But I did. I wish I hadn't.

That was the last I saw of that double-barrel BB gun for over a year. I lost it the same day I got it. A year later, I didn't care much to own it. Responsibility comes with a price tag. He had tried to tell me. Had I listened, I wouldn't be telling you this story today. My father and his brown leather belt helped keep the memory alive. Looking back, I would take that whipping all over again just for the chance to tell him he was right. He almost always was right.

The memory of that experience keeps me in mind of this passage:

> A wise son responds to his father's discipline, but a
> mocker doesn't listen to rebuke. (Prov. 13:1)

My father, on the other hand, probably had a different verse in mind on that Christmas morning in 1940:

Foolishness is tangled up in the heart of a youth; but
the rod of discipline will drive it away from him.
(Prov. 22:15)

Discipline was a prominent feature of my upbringing. On
occasion it involved punishment. Sometimes it required my mother's switch, and on rare occasions my father's brown belt. Once, in
an act of youthful defiance, I yanked the switch from my mother's
hand, and declared that I was too old to get any more whippings.
My grandfather was living with us at the time. He was a tough old
German, and he grabbed me, took the switch from my hand and
held me over his knee while my mother applied it to my bottom.
I mentioned that I only tried that *once*, didn't I? I never had the
chutzpah to try it again. But, yes, I had a penchant for mischief
in my youth. I eventually learned, however, that others would
not need to discipline me if I learned to discipline myself. By the
time I grew too big to spank, the need for such punishment had
diminished. Self-discipline kicked in. I realized that self-discipline
allowed me to discover much more happiness and contentment
than a lack of discipline ever could. Its lessons have carried me
through a lifetime.

Most of the discipline my parents enforced had nothing to do
with punishment and everything to do with the lifestyle they were
striving for. Let me offer an abbreviated list of the disciplines that
were regularly imposed during my childhood:

- Weekly church attendance with my parents
- Regular tithing at church
- Family meals at breakfast and supper
- Family prayer before each meal and individual prayer at
  bedtime

- Regular Bible study
- Clean, non-vulgar language
- Completion of household chores
- Proper behavior at social functions
- No alcohol consumption or smoking
- Nightly curfews
- Attend school unless too sick to attend (and if too sick to attend, then "stay in bed all day and, NO, you may not go out to play with friends after school lets out!")
- Homework and study each school night
- Get outside work if you want spending money
- Show respect to your parents
- Show respect to elders
- Do not mistreat girls and *never* hit a girl
- Work hard
- Don't be a quitter
- Don't complain; rather, look for the positives
- Stick to your commitments
- Do your best
- Tell the truth
- Be kind to people
- Obey God above all

My parents didn't merely impose these rules. They lived them. As a small boy, I found their rules onerous. My father, the banker-turned-real-estate broker, sang in the church choir on Sundays. My mother taught an adult Sunday school class. I can't tell you how many Sunday mornings I quietly laid in bed hoping my parents might oversleep and miss church. They never did. Only once in their lives did they drink alcohol. It was at a banker's convention shortly after the martini craze was invented, sometime in the

1930s. After that experience, they never drank anything stronger than coffee or tea. For my part, I have never tasted an alcoholic beverage. As a child I heard bad stories about alcohol abuse. Even had a few friends whose parents had drinking problems. It was a common phenomenon among veterans who had recently returned from the war in Europe and Asia. As a man, the opportunity was presented often. I always refused. My biggest fear was that I might try it and like it. No sense going down that path, I reasoned. Coaching and family life brought enough pressures. Why try to deal with them through a haze?

As I got older and started a family of my own, I came to realize why my parents had imposed such discipline upon me. They did it because they loved me. They wanted me to discover the power of self-control. They wanted me to be safe and self-confident and empowered to say NO to myself when YES would lead to trouble. More important, they wanted me to say Yes to God. They knew they would not always be there for me. The day would come when the decisions were left solely to me. Would my decisions be good ones? They asked themselves that question long before the answer ever mattered to me.

Time went by. My life blossomed. Theirs faded. I grew up and came to see the world through their eyes. I saw my children as my parents once saw me—through eyes that look beyond a child's youth into the life that comes after. My wife and I loved our children from the beginning. Therefore discipline was inescapable. True love and discipline are inseparable. Fortunately for me, my parents practiced what they preached. Their rules may have been nonnegotiable, but they applied the rules to themselves as much as to me, and they were consistent in the application. "No" meant "no" regardless of how much I pleaded or cajoled. They loved me with a constancy that I could not fully appreciate as a child. Now I know. I see what they saw. It has carried me through a lifetime. So I pass along to you what was passed along to me. Self-discipline lies at the heart of all good loving and good living. It's something one must experience in order to truly understand. Training for it is best done in youth. But any time is a good time to begin.

The discipline instilled in me by my parents is but the echo of lessons learned millennia ago by our ancestors. From the earliest days of biblical literature to the latest, such wisdom already was being passed down from one generation to the next:

> Honor your father and your mother so that you
> may have a long life in the land that the LORD your
> God is giving you. (Exod. 20:12)

> Do not despise the LORD's instruction, my son, and
> do not loathe His discipline; for the LORD disci-
> plines the one He loves, just as a father, the son he
> delights in. (Prov. 3:11–12)

> Teach a youth about the way he should go;
> even when he is old he will not depart from it.
> (Prov. 22:6)

> Fathers, don't stir up anger in your children, but
> bring them up in the training and instruction of the
> Lord. (Eph. 6:4)

As always, it is prudent to remember that these biblical insights were hard-won lessons. Did our ancestors try alternative methods of parenting, such as overindulgence . . . abusiveness . . . neglect

. . . or indifference to moral training? Of course they did. Time and again. I doubt there are any theories of parenting today that haven't been tried over and over again through the millennia. And always the same painful lessons are learned as a result. Scripture offers the distilled wisdom of people who discovered how best to raise their children—namely, in the fear and knowledge of the Living God. The best path for parents is not easy and often is not fun. But it leads to a happiness far more enduring for the effort.

The difference between fun and happiness is more than semantic. Everyone loves to have fun. I know I do. But fun is transient. It comes and goes. Whenever my team got up big on another team early, the rest of the game was usually fun, as any fan will tell you. My best rounds of golf are fun. Telling a joke is fun. I delight in the experience as it occurs. Unfortunately, the quest for happiness is not a continuously euphoric experience. Indeed, the quest can lead through moments of great pain. I've never met a mother who said that childbirth—or the sleepless nights spent tending a colicky newborn—was fun. No football player thinks two-a-day practices in the August heat is fun. Nor a medical student who must work sleepless nights as an intern in the hospital emergency room. Indeed, few of the endeavors that lead to success and happiness are inherently fun experiences. Imagine a parent saying, "I decided to quit taking care of my child because it wasn't fun anymore."

Happiness lies at the end of a long and sometimes difficult road. It's an uphill journey at first. We often want to quit. But the road begins to level out and then bends down and the journey becomes much more satisfying. Self-discipline helps get us to that point.

Some think that self-discipline results in little more than a boring, joyless, and non-adventurous life. Nothing could be farther from the truth. The ability to say No to ourselves—or No to temptation—is, in fact, essential to a happy and contented life. People who are in control of their lives enjoy a much higher level of satisfaction than those who are buffeted daily by problems that could have been avoided with a little self-discipline. Indeed, I think self-loathing, defeatism, discontent, and chronic misery often result from the *lack* of self-discipline. Either we conquer our bad habits or they conquer us.

People who practice self-discipline are more liberated than those who cannot regulate their desires. Desire is not bad in and of itself. But unregulated desire is slavery at heart. If the satisfaction of desire mattered most to me, my diet certainly would be different today. I would eat all the foods I like when I wanted them. I'm thinking lasagna and French bread several nights a week, a double helping, followed by chocolate pie for dessert, except for the nights when I topped apple cobbler with a big dollop of ice cream, followed the next morning with donuts and coffee for breakfast, a milkshake every afternoon, and treats like banana pudding and fudge brownies whenever my appetite kicked in between meals. Yes, those are my epicurean fantasies. I love chocolate so much that it doesn't have to love me back. Your desires may differ. Unfortunately, if I indulged those fantasies, I would be dead right now. One could say the same for all areas of life. Too much of a good thing can lead to painful consequences. Slavery to bad health, for instance, or the sacrifice of self-esteem, or both. That kind of freedom is hardly desirable. Is it really freedom at all?

I went through a period, years ago, when I would gain weight and then lose it, then gain it back and need to lose it again. I felt miserable when I overate and miserable when I had to diet. An added dose of self-discipline mostly freed me from that cycle of miseries. Some people go through a similar misery when they spout off in anger, then must apologize, then spout off again, followed by yet another apology. Lacking self-control, we find ourselves in bondage to our moods, hungers, passions, and all the consequences of our bad decisions. A person whose life is under control is liberated from those hurtful cycles.

That's why Paul could say:

> No discipline seems enjoyable at the time, but pain-
> ful. Later on, however, it yields the fruit of peace
> and righteousness to those who have been trained
> by it. (Heb. 12:11)

The *peaceful fruit of righteousness* is itself a revealing phrase. Righteousness has to do with our relationships with people and with nature itself. To be righteous in the biblical sense means to manage our relationships rightly or properly. Life is a web of relationships. We have relationships with spouses, children, neighbors, friends, acquaintances, coworkers, lenders, clients, shopkeepers, and so forth. Each of those relationships involves a different set of rights and obligations. I have one set of obligations to my spouse, a different set of obligations to my employees, and yet another to the bank that holds my mortgage. If I meet my various obliga-tions—satisfy my financial commitments, show fidelity to my spouse, treat my employees fairly—I am acting righteously in the biblical sense. Through such righteous actions I find satisfaction

and self-respect. It is never easy to fulfill our various responsibilities. But as we discipline ourselves to meet those obligations, says
Paul, we find that it yields the "fruit of peace." Strife decreases.
Happiness, peace, and contentment increase. Who in their right
mind would not want that trinity?

The only obstacle in our path is . . . ourselves.

Inwardly we are embroiled in a tug-of-war. An inner conflict
pits our natural desires against our own best interests. Who in
their right mind would undercut their own contentment in life?
Who in their right mind would fail to practice self-control if their
happiness depended on it? *All of us,* says the Bible. You and me
and everyone else. Such was Paul's meaning when he wrote:

> For I do not do the good that I want to do,
> but I practice the evil that I do not want to do.
> (Rom. 7:19)

Divided inwardly, we become our own worst enemies. It is
not surprising that we have such difficulty getting along with others when we cannot even get along with ourselves. The problem
isn't due to a lack of intelligence or vision. We all can see what is
needed to make life better. We just can't manage to make it better.
We know what we should do. Yet so often we choose otherwise.
And therein lies the rub. It has everything to do with this conflict
that roils within us. Until we make peace with ourselves, we will
never live in harmony with others.

The struggle to find such peace and happiness—and the self-
discipline needed to maintain it—lies at the intersection of agony
and the Living God.

Why agony? Because we who wish to find ourselves first must lose ourselves. We must die to self and live to God. And we must choose to do this daily.

The dying part involves learning to say No to ourselves. In the biblical meaning, this No is not some joyless act of self-denial or asceticism. Rather, it is aimed toward a goal—the "pearl of great price" (Matt. 13:46 NKJV) that we yearn to have for ourselves. And it is not passive. The No spoken in faith is tenacious . . . determined . . . and fierce. Above all, it is life-affirming. It is the kind of No we say when we resolve never to revisit a place that brings us only pain and misery. It is the kind of No we say to an adversary when we determine that "No, you will never triumph over me!" Ultimately, it is the No we proclaim daily as we fight to seek and know the Living God. It is to ourselves that we first must speak this word.

Saying No to ourselves is not easy to do. The New Testament speaks often about striving to know the Living God. The Greek word for *striving is agonizomenos.* You recognize immediately the word *agony*, which indicates that striving includes distress. Indeed, it involves pain and sacrifice. The Greek word *agonizomenos* is described in Scripture as *fighting, contending, struggling, wrestling, pummeling, laboring,* and *running to the point of exhaustion.* These words help explain the "agony" of discipleship. Discipleship requires grit and determination, a sometimes exhausting resolve to win the race. But we do not strive alone or in vain. Each step of the way, the Living God is there to inspire and strengthen us for victory.

Observe the imagery as Paul describes his experience of *agonizomenos*:

Don't you know that the runners in a stadium all
race, but only one receives the prize? Run in such a
way to win the prize. Now everyone who competes
exercises self-control in everything. However, they
do it to receive a crown that will fade away, but we
a crown that will never fade away. Therefore I do
not run like one who runs aimlessly or box like one
beating the air. Instead, I discipline my body and
bring it under strict control, so that after preaching
to others, I myself will not be disqualified. (1 Cor.
9:24–27)

I labor for this, striving with His strength that works
powerfully in me. (Col. 1:29)

In this same vein, Paul counsels his young colleague Timothy:

Fight the good fight for the faith; take hold of
eternal life that you were called to and have made a
good confession about in the presence of many wit-
nesses. (1 Tim. 6:12)

And again, when writing to believers in Ephesus, Paul speaks
of discipleship in terms of war:

This is why you must take up the full armor of God,
so that you may be able to resist in the evil day, and
having prepared everything, to take your stand.
Stand, therefore, with truth like a belt around your
waist, righteousness like armor on your chest, and
your feet sandaled with readiness for the gospel of
peace. In every situation take the shield of faith, and

with it you will be able to extinguish all the flaming arrows of the evil one. Take the helmet of salvation, and the sword of the Spirit, which is God's Word. (Eph. 6:13–17)

Fight. Take hold. Struggle. Run. Box. Gird for battle. That's how Paul understood the experience of a faith that strives for God. That's the life of discipleship . . . of self-discipline. Nothing about it is passive. Believers do not agonize in any sense that suggests they wring their wrists in despair or sit by idly waiting to be made happy. Rather, they are agonists . . . strivers. They strive for a goal that gets nearer with each act of self-discipline. The apostle Paul, once again:

> Not that I have already reached the goal or am already fully mature, but I make every effort to take hold of it because I also have been taken hold of by Christ Jesus. Brothers, I do not consider myself to have taken hold of it. But one thing I do: Forgetting what is behind and reaching forward to what is ahead, I pursue as my goal the prize promised by God's heavenly call in Christ Jesus. (Phil. 3:12–14)

Such striving allowed Paul to raise his head high and proclaim victory at the end. The *agonizomenos*—the striving—was worth the effort. Toward the end of his life, in his second letter to young Timothy, Paul offered these parting words:

> I have fought the good fight, I have finished the race, I have kept the faith. There is reserved for me in the future the crown of righteousness, which the

Lord, the righteous Judge, will give me on that day,
and not only to me, but to all those who have loved
His appearing. (2 Tim. 4:7–8)

The fruits of a disciplined faith translate directly into our public and professional lives. Through discipline we get the most out of what we have. I have been very fortunate as a football coach. My coaches, players, and I shared in one of college football's most historic and successful winning streaks. In the decade of the 1990s, we won more football games than any other Division I school, posting a cumulative record of 110–13–1. The team won undisputed national championships in 1993 and 1999, and we played for three other championships during that stretch. We finished in the Top 5 for fourteen consecutive years between 1987 and 2000, and played in New Year's Day bowls for fifteen consecutive seasons. On behalf of the team and coaches, I received a number of honors during that stretch, along with others that came afterward. The most humbling of all honors came in 2006 when I received the National Football Foundation's Gold Medal Award. Past recipients include seven U.S. presidents, four generals, three admirals, a Supreme Court justice, and baseball great Jackie Robinson, many of whom were heroes of mine during childhood and beyond. I mention these events only to reinforce that what I say next has been tried and tested and proven true to my lasting satisfaction—namely, that discipline is essential to success in one's career and in one's life. I witnessed it. I participated in it. I made it central to my program. And I have no doubt about it.

When I first arrived at Florida State in 1976, the team had been through some rough times, winning only four games the previous three seasons. Fan attendance had dropped off significantly. As

I often said during public speeches in those days, whenever fans called the office and asked what time kickoff was on Saturday, I usually responded, "What time can you get here?" Seriously, though, I discovered shortly after my arrival in Tallahassee that the players had grown accustomed to losing. They didn't know what it felt like to be winners and, quite frankly, a few of them didn't care. Nothing is more disheartening to a coach than to see talent wasted through lack of self-discipline. I had to put several starters on the bench and dismiss a few others before they understood how I wanted things done. Before the year was out, they were listening much better. We won five games that first season. The next year, 1977, we won ten games, which included a bowl victory over Texas Tech. The boys got a taste of winning and—guess what?—they liked it. Winning felt much better than losing. They wanted more of it. They suddenly felt more in control of their own destiny. But to continue winning, discipline was needed. More specifically, self-discipline. They would need to continue striving for the goal with just as much determination as the year before. No slacking off. They had to stay hungry.

And they did. We practiced and practiced and practiced until finally the things they were practicing became habits. Like the military recruit who is forced to disassemble and reassemble his rifle until he can do it blindfolded, my players hit the field with newfound self-confidence rooted in habits that improved their performance. Curiously, the hard work didn't seem as onerous as before. Self-discipline created opportunities that a lack of discipline never would. Two years later those same players went undefeated in the regular season, climbed to a #4 ranking in the national poll and played Oklahoma in the 1979 Orange Bowl. Each year afterward, when a new crop of freshmen came in, the older players set the standard and let the young guys know what was expected of them. Those boys never lost their taste for winning. They still haven't. In fact, FSU hasn't had a losing season since my first year there in 1976.

You don't have to believe me, but I will say it anyway: no one finds success and fulfillment without self-discipline. Happiness doesn't happen by accident. It is given by grace as a gift from God to all who *strive* for it through obedience to His will. The motivation for striving (*agonizomenos*) is the misery of losing. One needs only a little taste of victory—a taste of what life can be—to want more of it. The benefit of striving is not so much what we get from it as who we become as a result. It is ourselves that we are fighting for—our happiness, our inner peace, and sense of purpose. We want to be free of the conflicts that plague us inwardly. We want some better way than what we have found on our own. God knows this. He always has known this. His response is terse and simple:

"I stand at the door and knock. . . ." (Rev. 3:20)

To answer the door is to be invited on a journey.
It is the journey of discipleship.

CHAPTER 8

THE WISDOM
of CONTENTMENT

Contentment is a feast without end.

(Prov. 15:15 translated by Rabbi Meir Leibush)

I never wanted to do anything but coach football for a living. I got the itch as a teenager. Call me naïve, but the way things looked at the time, coaching was one of those jobs where people ask, "Do you actually get paid for doing this?"

So that's what I did. Had I been unsuccessful in those early years, I probably would have scrapped around for another coaching job just to stay in the game. Only two things would have driven me away—either the best interests of my family, or my own inability. Few of us ever know if we are good at something until we give it an earnest try. I owe most of my success to my wife. She never expected me to be the best. But she did expect me to be good enough. And she kept raising the bar!

I did not make much money in the first twenty years. No sane person goes into coaching for the money. Or for job security. You do it because you love the game and want to be part of it. Or else because you're not very smart! The wages of a beginning coach are embarrassingly low. Only a relatively small number of coaches—all at the major college level—earn the kind of money that can "wow" you. Yet even among them, the turnover rate is high. A coach who is on top one year can be on his way out the next. The moves add up quickly. My family was lucky. We only moved five times while the children were growing up, and after 1976 I didn't need to move again. Fortunately, all my moves were up the ladder. Most major college coaches and their families move about six to ten times in a career. The moves are often involuntary. Incomes can fluctuate dramatically from one job to the next. Major college coaching is a feast-*and*-famine profession. In the transition from one job to the next, retirement vestment periods often don't get satisfied, bridge loans may be needed until the old house is sold and a new one purchased, savings accounts can get plundered to cover expenses, and one's spouse and children must make whatever adjustments are needed. It's a tough way to make a living. Worries can mount up in a hurry, and more so if your team isn't winning. The nagging questions are usually the same as for everyone: *If I lose this job, how will I pay the mortgage? . . . or put bread on the table? . . . or buy school supplies and make the car payment?* The coaching profession is a breeding ground for anxiety and discontent. I advised all my sons to consider careers outside of coaching. "Do not get into coaching unless you can't live without it," I said. Three of them ignored me.

In the Sermon on the Mount, Jesus speaks to all who are anxious about daily needs, who fret that material conditions first must be satisfied before we ever can hope to find satisfaction and contentment. That's the operative equation for most of us. Jesus simply reverses it. He challenges us to put last things first and work from there. Listen:

> "Don't worry about your life, what you will eat or
> what you will drink; or about your body, what you
> will wear. Isn't life more than food and the body
> more than clothing? . . . But seek first the kingdom
> of God and His righteousness, and all these things
> will be provided for you." (Matt. 6:25, 33)

I mention this passage of Scripture because I turned to it often, in older life as well as younger, but especially in the early decades of my coaching career, as I wrestled with the issue of contentment and peace of mind. There were a lot of things I struggled to provide in those days. Food, clothing, and shelter were prominent among them. My wife and I took extra jobs to make ends meet. I often grew anxious about my responsibility as a provider. Jesus challenged me to keep my focus on God—seek His will first and foremost in all I do—and allow the rest to work out as it will. That's a big pill to swallow. The monthly bills didn't simply disappear when I turned to the pages of Scripture. But Jesus' words became a refuge for me. I learned to find peace and contentment in them.

It wasn't easy. My wife and I married at an early age. I was nineteen. She was sixteen. We secretly eloped one Saturday morning in April 1948, when my parents were out of town at a banking conference. They took a train to Atlanta and left the car in the garage. Seizing the opportunity, I borrowed the car and twenty dollars from a friend, picked up Ann at her house early that morning, drove east across the Georgia line, stopped in a roadside town called Rising Fawn, and paid a justice of the peace for a simple marriage ceremony. I got Ann back to her house that afternoon before any suspicions were raised. The wedding cost five dollars. The remaining fifteen was spent on a speeding ticket, gas, and a honeymoon lunch of sandwiches and iced tea. That's all we had time for. It was a whirlwind ordeal. Come Sunday, neither of our parents had an inkling of what we had done. Ann and I believed we had reached the pinnacle of contentment—she living at home with her parents, me with mine, yet both of us secretly bound by a lifetime commitment. News of our clandestine operation got out a few months later. Turns out our blabbermouth friends at school were no better at keeping secrets than Ann and I. Our parents soon got wind of it. Neither household was happy— except for Ann and me. We were happy as jaybirds. Little did we know that we had just completed the easy part. Contentment proved a bit more elusive than we first imagined.

Eight years later, when I was twenty-seven, Ann and I packed our bags and headed toward my first head football coaching job at South Georgia College. We carried three children with us, ages five, four, and two. We knew going in that money would be tight. The job paid only $4,200 a year. To fit housing expenses into our budget, we rented a former officers' barracks on an abandoned military base. The base had been decommissioned after World War II, and the empty barracks were opened up for rent to the public. The barracks we selected had two small bedrooms in the back, a modest living room and kitchenette just inside the front door, and a bathroom in-between that included several toilets and sinks and a walk-in shower. The floor was slab concrete, painted gray. We put newspapers on the floor during the coldest days of winter to help absorb the condensation. My children never seemed to mind. They thought we were rich. None of their friends at school had multiple sinks and toilets in a single bathroom, much less an open walk-in shower with two showerheads!

Ann and I did what we could to make ends meet. We worked long hours, bought off-brands at the grocery, persuaded football players to volunteer for babysitting duty, passed down clothing from one child to the next, and otherwise got the most from every penny we earned. Pennies were scarce. We stretched them as far as we could. Or so I thought.

Not long after we settled in, Ann decided our daughter needed piano lessons. The *need* happened to coincide with the arrival of a piano instructor several barracks down from us. Ann made the mistake of discussing it with me in advance. With a gentle and consoling smile on my face (which is how I prefer to remember the conversation), I begged to differ on the definition of *need*, then went on to explain that we couldn't afford piano lessons or any other indulgence at that point—which she well knew—and, anyway, we didn't own a piano. I could see her eyes drifting away as I summarized our financial constraints. Her distant look should have been a clue. I now realize what was going on. She was privately negotiating a settlement of our differences on the piano. More specifically, she was conceding the logic of my argument, but at the same time she was adding up all the money we were going to save by *not* paying for piano lessons, then reasoning that there might be enough "saved money" in the deal to buy a piano after all. I wish she had included me in the negotiations. When I was at work the next week, she went downtown and used our "saved money" to buy a piano on credit. Her explanation was simple and, in part, irrefutable: "The installment payments cost less per month than piano lessons. And on top of that, the first payment isn't due for two months." Thus began the first of many lively discussions we've had over the years, all of which seem to revolve around Venus and Mars. Time heals old wounds, of course. Almost sixty years have passed since that disagreement over the piano. I rarely bring it up anymore!

Before I get too far afield from the subject of contentment, I will tell one more story about Ann that helps explain her strong and determined personality. Ann was a beautiful young woman. I wasn't the only person to notice. She received many such compliments over the years. When we moved into that military barracks in 1956, we didn't have a washer and dryer and the stove was dilapidated. Ann opened the newspaper one day and noticed an advertisement for the Mrs. Georgia beauty pageant. It was similar to statewide competition for the Miss America pageant, except this one was for married women. There would be preliminary competition to select Mrs. North Georgia and Mrs. South Georgia. A statewide winner would then be chosen between the two. Ann didn't have any interest in beauty pageants per se. What caught her eye was the prize awarded to Mrs. South Georgia—a new washer and dryer, which we couldn't afford but she was determined to have. Long story short, Ann entered that competition and won the Mrs. South Georgia title. Once she collected her winnings, she renounced her crown and dropped out of the contest. I never met a woman more proud of washing clothes for her family. She would have made one tough CEO had the times been different. By the way, if you want to know how she ended up getting a new stove as well, just stop and calculate how much "saved money" Ann now had available by not having to buy a washer and dryer and . . . well, you can figure out the rest. She's always been smarter than me.

I tell these stories to acknowledge that our lives were typical of most young couples who struggle to make ends meet. We found plenty of reasons to emote, fight, brood, worry, withdraw, and stay awake at night. The strain was intense at times. I remain thankful that we committed to put God first despite the struggles we wrestled with. Church attendance played a vital role. When we found ourselves threatening to veer off course, our involvement in the local church kept us on track. Sermons helped. Bible study too. But the greater value came from fellowship with others who shared the same vision of life and made the same commitments to God that Ann and I had made. Being in church reminded us that the workaday world was only one dimension of life, and not the most important dimension at that. Sitting beside other believers reminded us that we were meant for better things. Our sights were meant to be set higher. And thus God kept us true to our oaths—and in love with one another—by lifting us above our narrow interests. *Keep your eyes on Me,* God told us each week, *and these other things will take care of themselves.* This book is my testimony to the truth of the Living God.

With God's help, I've now been happily married for nearly four decades. That's not bad considering Ann and I have been married over sixty years! Yes, that's a joke. My point is that life is never perfect. Those who think contentment means we should be happy every moment and in every circumstance miss the point of contentment. There is a lot to be discontented with on any given day. Jesus Himself acknowledged as much when He told His disciples:

> "Therefore don't worry about tomorrow, because
> tomorrow will worry about itself. Each day has
> enough trouble of its own." (Matt. 6:34)

Today's trouble may dog us from dawn 'til dusk. Some days are like that. And sometimes an entire football season can be like that. Yet those troubles take on a different meaning against the backdrop of God's sovereignty over life. Jesus challenges us to take that perspective. *One day at a time,* He advises. *Keep your eyes on God. Obey Him. Trust Him. Make the pledge. Then do your best. Otherwise your burdens will overwhelm you and misery will set in.* Jesus spoke from experience. Races are won not by those who count the steps but by those who envision victory and strain for the finish line. If only we dared to put the Living God before all else. Contentment could be ours. That was Paul's experience, too. In his letter to the church in Rome—a congregation that faced hardship and oppression daily—he aimed to inspire them with a question:

> Who can separate us from the love of Christ? Can
> affliction or anguish or persecution or famine or
> nakedness or danger or sword? (Rom. 8:35)

Those were existential questions for believers in Rome. Roman policy makers were tolerant of all kinds of religious sects except those who refused to pledge ultimate loyalty to the Roman Empire. Nearly two thousand years later, Adolph Hitler rose to power in Germany and proclaimed *Deutschland über alles*—Germany first and foremost! Woe unto any German citizen who didn't profess loyalty to Hitler's Nazi regime. Believers in Rome found themselves in a similar circumstance. The Empire demanded everyone's ultimate allegiance. But the believers in Rome held fast to their profession that the Living God is sovereign above all, even above the Empire. Without specifically saying it, Paul who is more powerful—the throne of Rome or the throne of God?—and he answered his own question with a defiant assertion:

> No, in all these things we are more than victorious
> through Him who loved us. For I am persuaded
> that not even death or life, angels or rulers, things
> present or things to come, hostile powers, height
> or depth, or any other created thing will have the
> power to separate us from the love of God that is in
> Christ Jesus our Lord! (Rom. 8:37–39)

That, my friends, is conviction in the sovereignty of the Living God. And what convinced him? What cemented such a triumphant exclamation in the face of imminent danger? The answer is simple. Experience. Years of experience. And not easy years at that. Life undoubtedly was difficult for believers who lived in the heart of the Roman Empire. Paul sympathized with their plight. But his life hadn't been a walk in the park either. Indeed, his steely resolve was forged on the anvil of incessant hardships and suffering. Listen to what he revealed in an earlier letter to the church in Corinth:

> Five times I received 39 lashes from Jews. Three
> times I was beaten with rods by the Romans. Once
> I was stoned by my enemies. Three times I was

shipwrecked. I have spent a night and a day in the open sea. On frequent journeys, I faced dangers from rivers, dangers from robbers, dangers from my own people, dangers from the Gentiles, dangers in the city, dangers in the open country, dangers on the sea, and dangers among false brothers; labor and hardship, many sleepless nights, hunger and thirst, often without food, cold, and lacking clothing. Not to mention other things, there is the daily pressure on me: my care for all the churches. Who is weak, and I am not weak? Who is made to stumble, and I do not burn with indignation? (2 Cor. 11:24–29)

Paul didn't just preach the faith. He lived it. Suffered for it. Proved it. Drew strength from it. And refused to relinquish it. Paul didn't bother going into detail with believers in Rome about the various sufferings he had endured. They probably knew those details already. Rather, he shared with them the one overarching lesson he learned throughout the process:

For I consider that the sufferings of this present time are not worth comparing with the glory that is going to be revealed to us. (Rom. 8:18)

As he writes the words, you can imagine Paul recollecting the many ordeals he has endured. His mind jumps from the whippings to the shipwreck to days without food. He looks back over them with pen in hand, and then he looks beyond them to the throne that rises above all earthly thrones, and the words flow naturally as he puts pen to page. To understand what contentment meant to the apostle Paul, it helps to think his thoughts as you read what flowed from his pen: *For I consider that the sufferings of this present time are not worthy. . . .*

We yearn to say something like that . . . and mean it. Paul doesn't want us simply to grasp the concept of contentment. He wants us to *experience* it. Faith challenges us to discover firsthand what it means to put our lives in God's keeping.

I came across several news articles recently that focused on the benefits of faith in God. One study concluded that faith is a great stress reliever. People with a firm belief in God, the researchers discovered, enjoy a sense of purpose that helps keep life in perspective; believers tend to be less focused on unimportant things and enjoy a high level of inner peace. Another study found that people who attend church regularly tend to commit fewer crimes and their children are less inclined toward delinquent behavior. Yet another found that the positive attitude of religious people enhances their ability to overcome illnesses. Some of these studies are reported under dramatic headlines, such as: *Shocker! New Research Suggests Faith in God Actually Helps.* Well, the headlines are not quite as dramatic as that, but such is often my impression when I read some news reports these days, as though a groundbreaking discovery has just been made. And perhaps for some it is a new discovery, something they never before imagined. But in fact the discovery has been an open secret for millennia.

Listen:

A tranquil heart is life to the body. (Prov. 14:30)

The Lord is my shepherd; there is nothing I lack. (Ps. 23:1)

The fear of the Lord leads to life; one will sleep at
night without danger. (Prov. 19:23)

But everything that was a gain to me, I have considered to be a loss because of Christ. More than that,
I also consider everything to be a loss in view of the
surpassing value of knowing Christ Jesus my Lord.
Because of Him I have suffered the loss of all things
and consider them filth, so that I may gain Christ.
(Phil. 3:7–8)

I have made a journey that young people are just now setting
out on. They venture onto roads that I travelled long ago. Life
was all ahead of me in those days. My convictions had yet to be
battle tested. The future was little more than fantasy. These days
I can glance in the rearview mirror of life and still see the figure
of young Bobby Bowden, the kid who wanted nothing more
than to be a football coach. My forehead is now creased with a
lifetime of lessons, my eyes more informed and reflective. I see
things that the young boy in my rearview mirror couldn't yet see
. . . wasn't yet old enough to understand, or perhaps could have
better understood had he not rushed right past them. The Living
God has proven Himself to me, not once or twice but steadfastly,
through good times and bad. The dreams I had in youth have
undergone many revisions. Circumstances took me in directions
I did not anticipate. The landscape changed, challenges took on
different shapes, and I ended up in places that the boy in the
mirror never expected to be. Yet the steadfastness of God always
proved true. I don't pretend that faith is a placebo. Sufferings and
misfortunes don't magically disappear just because we believe in
God. Sometimes they become more intense. What changes is the

way we handle those difficulties. Faith is a wise guide. It gives us a perspective that makes contentment real.

I cannot count how many nights I came home from work discouraged or disappointed. There were at least 124 different occasions. That's how many games I lost in my career, not counting the four ties. Player problems, staffing issues, exhausting hours, and frequent nights away from home sometimes far overshadowed the game itself. God enabled me to keep life in perspective throughout the process. He allowed me—indeed, He demanded me—to let go of worries over which I had no control and let Him guide me through the rest. I've tried to do that to the best of my abilities. People who know me well have joked about my ability to sleep just about anywhere at any time. There's truth to the joke. When I would get on an airplane, I could fall asleep shortly after buckling my seat belt and stay asleep until the plane landed. Even if I was being driven to a speaking engagement forty minutes away, I could sleep in the passenger seat for thirty-eight minutes of the trip. Back at the office, my secretary knew not to forward any phone calls during my noontime "power naps." Some of my sleep habits were due to the busy schedule I kept while at FSU, needing to grab sleep whenever I could. But the bigger reason is that I learned to leave my cares in God's hands. I could close my eyes and rest in Him. And I did. Every chance I got!

It's interesting to reflect back over one's life and ask, *When was I the happiest, the most contented?* The answer for me is one that you might not expect. Yes, I have enjoyed winning national championships. Being a winner is fun when you're winning. Fame is much the same. I no longer worry about putting bread on the table or keeping a roof over my head. Those issues have long been resolved. Yet the happiest days of my life may well have been those younger years in Douglas, Georgia, when Ann and I struggled mightily to make ends meet. Pocket change was about the only extra money we had in those days. We had four children to feed, clothe, and raise. All of our worldly possessions—except for that dadgum new piano!—could have been fit into a small trailer and towed behind our tattered station wagon.

No one would have mistaken us for the Howells on *Gilligan's Island*. But guess what? Douglas, Georgia, had something that one can rarely find these days—a drive-in movie theater! Most small towns had one back in the 1950s. Drive-ins were basically a gravel parking lot with a movie screen on one end and a concession stand on the other. In between were parking spaces with individual speakers that could be mounted on the car window. And guess what else? The cost of a drive-in movie was little more than pocket change! That was just the right price for couples as broke as us. So on warm Friday nights in the summer, Ann and I would dress the children in their pajamas, load them into the station wagon, and head down Ocilla Road toward the Skyview drive-in theater. About the time the gravel settled under our tires, the children would scramble onto the roof of the station wagon with blankets in hand and watch the movie from up there. They giggled and ate popcorn and eventually fell asleep. Meanwhile, Ann and I sat shoulder-to-shoulder in the front seat and enjoyed a peaceful evening. Thirty-three years later, cameras flashed all around as I stood with my team in the Oval Office of the White House. FSU had just won the national championship. I was making more money than I ever dreamed a coach could earn. Our children—six in all—were grown and gone. The kind of worries that plagued us daily in those early years had dissipated like vapor in the wind. But if you ask me when Ann and I were the most contented, the happiest, and most at peace, I think back to those years when we had so little. What could be better than sitting beneath the stars at the Skyview with a loving wife at my side and four sleepy children on the roof? And for nothing more than pocket change!

So how much is enough? How much *stuff* does it take to be content? I believe the wisest and most content people are those who have discovered the virtue of simplicity. They measure contentment by a yardstick unrelated to material goods. And thus they are liberated to experience dimensions of life that remain hidden from fools and the misdirected. We err if we think anyone can wrest contentment from the things of this world. Those are not my words. They are words from the Living God. Human experience is but the confirmation of them.

It's usually not until life becomes complicated that we find ourselves yearning for the joy of simplicity. We want to draw a deep relaxing breath and say, "I am content with my life just the way it is." And we want to feel that way not just for the moment but for the whole of our lives—for better or worse, in sickness and in health, rich or poor, whatever life may bring. To have such a longing is good. To satisfy it is joy. But to get there, great wisdom is needed. Such wisdom comes only from faith.

Simplicity does not require us to abandon the world and go nomad. I am as suspicious of those who preach against prosperity as I am those who preach a prosperity gospel. There is no one-size-fits-all lifestyle required—or promised—by faith.

The virtue of simplicity challenges us to focus on what is necessary and liberate ourselves from what is unnecessary. A cluttered life is not a sign of achievement. Life gets complicated all by itself. We complicate it further by confusing needs with wants.

Subtly, almost imperceptibly, we start believing that contentment isn't possible until we get what we want. And *wants* tend to be defined in terms of money and material possessions, or whatever else "successful people" have that we don't have. Not that wanting or having material things is evil. Not by a long shot. Money isn't evil, either. The apostle Paul reminded young Timothy that

> . . . the love of money is a root of all kinds of evils.
> (1 Tim. 6:10)

That is so true. And good advice. But note that it is the *love* of money, not money itself, that Paul warns about. By love, he means a commitment to money that surpasses one's commitment to the Living God. He says that such love produces "all kinds of" evils, not all evil. Money in itself is no more the cause of evil than food is the cause of gluttony.

A number of admirable characters in Scripture enjoyed material wealth. Abraham, David, Solomon, Job, the author of Ecclesiastes, and such prophets as Isaiah and Daniel were people of means. Many others had almost no earthly goods. Think of Moses, Jesus, and John the Baptist. Still others faced dire poverty. What they all came to discover is that material possessions are not the true measure of wealth. Nor are possessions the pathway to contentment. True wealth is measured not by what we have but by how little we need . . . to be happy.

Many people get halfway down the pathway of making this discovery for themselves. Then, when they see where the pathway might lead, they refuse to follow it any farther. They confess honestly and with a sigh of disgust, "I know I shouldn't complain, because I don't need any more than I have right now . . .", but you can tell by their tone of voice that they aren't willing to finish the thought. They don't want to own up to their own confession. *I am so tired of listening to you bellyache that I can hardly stand it!* we want to yell back in exasperation. *If you truly believe you don't need anything more to be happy, then why don't you just shut up and start living like you don't need more!* But we bite our tongue instead of responding so harshly, not out of courtesy but because we're standing in front of the bathroom mirror and it is ourselves that we are counseling! Advice is always easier when dished out to someone else.

Those who acquire much of anything in life eventually realize that there is a point of diminishing returns. At some point the value of our possessions is not worth the price we pay to have them. Shower a child with new toys each day and watch how quickly the child tires of them. Pick another child and repeat the experiment. Then do it again. The results don't vary. All that remains is to grasp the point of the experiment and apply it to ourselves. How much is enough? And how much is too much?

Each of us must decide this issue for ourselves. I don't know how to answer it for myself apart from faith in God. The more I see life through His eyes, the closer I come to an answer. Great joy can be found by those who have little and need less. Great joy can also be found by those who have much and give more. Contentment is available to us whatever our circumstance in life, if our eyes are set first and constantly on the Living God. Otherwise we keep trying to find in toys a value they don't have in them to give. Simplicity of lifestyle is an elegance—and a wealth—that can be enjoyed by rich and poor alike. It's not the amount of our possessions, but the value we give them, that distinguishes the wise from fools.

The hardest path to be on is to have more, not less. Jesus never seemed jealous of those who owned more than He did. He looked upon their possessions as something that could be of great service to God. Still, in the eyes of the Living God, those who have much are judged by a higher standard. The difference in expectation is because all the goods of this world belong not to us but to God Himself. He is jealous of the purposes for which we use them. Hence Jesus proclaimed:

> "Much will be required of everyone who has been
> given much. And even more will be expected of
> the one who has been entrusted with more." (Luke
> 12:48)

Jesus clearly recognized that some people are not gifted in the ways of worldly wealth. By dint of personality, choice, bias or misfortune, they will never run a Fortune 500 company or get pictured on *People* magazine. Some among them do not even know where tomorrow's meal will be found. "Blessed are the poor," Jesus said. Not just the poor in spirit but the *poor* poor, those who thirst for food and water. Jesus' thoughts rarely drifted from those who are denied any chance of improving their lives. *God has not forsaken you,* He assures them. *God's will for you shall prevail.* With His eyes still fixed on the poor, He then directed His voice to those who have more than they need. *You're in danger,* He tells them. *Do not forget that God has blessed you with skills and entrusted to you the oversight of His possessions. If you ignore His purposes, you put yourself in peril.* He framed the danger thusly:

"Again I tell you, it is easier for a camel to go
through the eye of a needle than for a rich person to
enter the kingdom of God." (Matt. 19:24)

He didn't exactly leave a lot of wiggle room on that one, did He? The danger is not in having things but in ignoring the One who really owns them. We are meant to tend the owner's vineyard. God help us if we forget the purpose for which our skills have been endowed and our services engaged. Not only will contentment be denied us, but there will be hell to pay when the owner returns. Jesus didn't mince words on the subject.

This will come as a disappointment to those who wish to engineer a utopian society, but there is no set quantum of life's goods that can make a person content. Even if there was, who gets to define what the "magic amount" is? Which expert gets anointed to draw the line between the *haves* and the *have nots*? Is it you? Me? Anyone who owns less stuff than we do? Shall we leave the decision to politicians? Economists? Trained psychologists? Or better yet to well-pedigreed intellectuals or young reformers fresh out of a lecture on social justice? I wouldn't trust any of them to define wealth or contentment for me. Not that they lack skills. There are lots of people with expertise in a great many areas. And they serve purposes that benefit society. But unless their advice on contentment is rooted in the ways of the Living God, I have little interest in their opinions on the subject.

Life's deepest issues are spiritual and existential. Dilemmas confront us without warning. Some are gut-wrenching and can rob our lives of meaning. The things we think matter most may end up mattering little on those occasions. Maybe today our problem is money. Then we get money but lose our health. Maybe the doctor helps us regain our health, but tragedy strikes and we are left grieving the loss of someone more precious than wealth or health. Or else some new problem arises that overshadows them all. What exactly is the prerequisite for contentment? Is it money? Health? Success? Fame? Job? Family? Reputation? Or perhaps some combination of them all? We're inclined to say Yes on that last one for obvious reasons. Why would God put us on earth otherwise? We were meant to enjoy His creation. And we are fools not to. I agree. The catch is that none of those things are guaranteed to us for as long as we want them or as much as we desire. Sin and human freedom have a lot to do with it. Plus the fact that we cannot see history the way God sees it. To Him a thousand years is like a day. It seems a thousand years ago since I last saw my parents and sister. God promises I will see them again. I'm not sure how to picture that reunion. But I live in the anticipation of it.

"The heart is restless," Augustine confessed, "until it finds its rest in Thee, O God." Such rest is the essence of contentment. Faith is the portal. It begins with a decision to follow Christ's lead. Obedience keeps us on track. In return, God gives us peace. It comes as an act of grace.

Such contentment must be learned over time. That's how Paul described it to his friends in Philippi:

> I have learned to be content in whatever circum-
> stances I am. I know both how to have a little, and
> I know how to have a lot. In any and all circum-
> stances I have learned the secret of being content—
> whether well fed or hungry, whether in abundance
> or in need. I am able to do all things through Him
> who strengthens me. (Phil. 4:11–13)

He wrote those words from inside a jail cell in Rome, penniless and destitute, quite a different ending from the career he imagined for himself as an aspiring young man. Some historians believe this letter to the church at Philippi was one of the last letters he ever wrote. He was put to death, they believe, shortly after sending the letter to Philippi by a messenger named Epaphroditus. Paul seems to have suspected that things would not end well for him. Yet, if he was anxious about dying, he hid it well. Perhaps he did what faith had taught him to do on so many other occasions—place his anxious heart in the hands of the Sovereign and Living God and let tomorrow work out as it will. That much seems clear to me in the passage cited above. His words are not those of a restless heart. His soul is calm and full of assurance. So he puts pen to paper and gives thanks for a seat at the banquet table of God.

His words echo a distant cry from the faith of his ancestors:

> Contentment is a feast without end.
> (Prov. 15:15 translated by Rabbi Meir Leibush)

CHAPTER 9

THE WISDOM
of SUFFERING

You will not grieve like the rest, who have no hope.

(1 Thess. 4:13)

This past December, my wife and I laid to rest another of our grandchildren. He died the night after Christmas. A car accident. Not far from his mother's house. He was twenty-three. Moments after my son Jeff learned of it, he called me with the news. "T. J. is dead," he said. No other words. Just those. Then a deep, heaving sigh. He was doing his best to finish the sentence. T. J. was his son.

Tragedy is surreal, like a nightmare that continues to dream itself long after we've awakened. Lines blur like they do at dusk when shadows surrender to darkness. The everyday world comes in and out of focus. The unthinkable becomes real. Then the real becomes unthinkable. We want to sleep again, if only to escape the moment. But we cannot. Instead, we find ourselves falling into a chasm. That chasm can swallow us whole if we let it. Or else faith can save us. And that's what we need when the ground opens beneath us. Salvation. Deliverance. The strong right hand of God. We need to feel the touch of His fingers, and then His arm around us, lifting us from the abyss.

That was Isaiah's discovery. I do not know what dark nights of the soul Isaiah endured in his lifetime. Nor do I know how many tears were needed to wash away his sorrow. The book that bears his name offers none of those details. But like Hosea, he understood suffering from the inside. The poignancy of his words is the clue. Those who suffer share a language all their own. Perhaps tragedy struck during his youth. Or maybe he lost a child or failed in some heartrending endeavor. I do not know. But listen to what he says about the Living God:

> He gives strength to the weary and strengthens the
> powerless. Youths may faint and grow weary, and
> young men stumble and fall, but those who trust
> in the LORD will renew their strength; they soar on
> wings like eagles; they will run and not grow weary;
> they will walk and not faint. (Isa. 40:29–31)

Ann and I sat beside Jeff at the funeral. All I could think of was how he was holding up. Was he finding sufficiency in the Living God? Was he finding the strength he needed? My daughter Ginger was nearby. She knew this moment only too well. Ten years earlier it was her son in the casket. Thirty years before that it was my sister Marion who died too young. I was in the car with her one afternoon as we drove to visit our mother, who was drifting into the late stages of Alzheimer's. Marion herself had terminal cancer. The pain already was severe. She knew her death was coming soon, probably before our mother died. We talked about it. And we talked about the Living God . . . the trust we put in Him . . . and the afterlife He promised. Marion and I shared the same confidence in God. Our lives were in His hands. She passed away soon afterward. Her husband and six children were at the funeral. Our mother, so ill, never knew about her daughter's death. I attended the funeral. Marion's departure left a great void in my life, even more so for her family. Yet I felt relieved for her. And glad in the faith we shared. Her suffering was over. She got to heaven before I did. And she was joined by our mother, who passed away shortly thereafter. I aim to see them again. And I am confident that God will make it so. The *how* of it is in His hands.

I marvel at the strength God gives us in our time of need. I understand what the psalmist must have experienced when he wrote:

> I will exalt You, Lord, because You have lifted me up . . . I cried to You for help, and You healed me. Lord, You brought me up from Sheol; You spared me from among those going down in the Pit. (Ps. 30:1–3)

In such moments we discover the meaning of other verses so familiar as to seem trite:

> For everyone who calls upon the name of the Lord will be saved. (Rom. 10:13)

To be saved is to experience deliverance *from* something. Isaiah speaks of those who "faint and grow weary," and who then "soar on wings like eagles." The psalmist speaks of being "lifted up" and of being "spared" from the pit. There are many ways to become lost. Suffering is always involved.

In the movie *Unforgiven*, Clint Eastwood's character, a reformed drunkard and cold-blooded killer named William Munny, lowers the barrel of his shotgun. Beneath him is the evil sheriff who tortured and whipped to death Munny's best friend. It's the revenge scene. The sheriff knows he cannot escape his fate. Yet he doesn't seem to fear the moment. Indeed, he has done a lot of killing himself, in cruel ways and often for unjust reasons. He knows his death will take only a second. And he knows it is coming. What bothers him most is the sheer humiliation of his circumstance. In his mind, he is a far more respectable man than his reprobate executioner, William Munny. How could such a lowlife be allowed to end his life? "I don't deserve to die like this," he says. That's when Munny scowls at him and utters the unforgettable line: "Deserve's got nothing to do with it."

The enigma of suffering comes down to those occasions when *deserve* has nothing to do with it. We experience many kinds of suffering in life. Much of it we bring upon ourselves, whether through folly or pride. We are then left to endure the consequences and come to terms with God. Some suffering we choose knowingly, or at least we consciously take the risk. I think of people who work dangerous jobs, or drive automobiles, or just about anyone who puts their trust in other fallible human beings. Relationships, like careers, come with risks we accept because of the rewards they promise. Suffering is one of those risks. Other types of suffering are part of life's normal cycle. As my doctor explained a few years ago when I was diagnosed with prostate cancer, the only men who don't die from prostate cancer are those who don't live long enough.

For the most part we endure such suffering with a grim nod to the wisdom of Ecclesiastes. He observed millennia ago that for everything there is a season. We accept certain kinds of suffering because to an extent we can make sense of them. Some types of suffering must be borne by just about everyone in some fashion—the heartache of betrayal, the loss of parents or brave soldiers, or the loss of health, wealth, or status. Such experiences are part and parcel of life.

Sometimes, however, the mantle of suffering falls upon us in a way that has nothing to do with "just desserts" or calculated risks or the normal cycles of life. During my high school days, the world was shocked to discover the atrocities committed in Hitler's death camps. Jewish citizens throughout Europe were rounded up, hauled off in cattle cars, and denied the least ounce of dignity. Once in the prison camp, they were stripped naked in front of their children, beaten, shot, raped, starved, fed to dogs, worked to death, experimented on without the benefit of anesthetics, and, for over six million of them, herded into concrete buildings where they were asphyxiated with poisonous gas. The cry went out worldwide: *How could such horrors be allowed to happen?* Especially among those who would soon die in the camps, the desperate cry must have been raised daily: *Why, O God, why?*

It would be heartless beyond words to suggest that Hitler's victims "had it coming." Deserve had nothing to do with it. Suffering can lead people to discover wellsprings of courage they never believed possible. It can reveal extraordinary levels of endurance. Or evoke unimagined heights of creativity. Great good can come from the most awful suffering. But that is no rationale for the suffering itself. Causes and effects must be carefully distinguished. It would be unspeakably callous to say that death camps and cancer-riddled children are God's way of teaching us a lesson. Nor should such suffering be explained as a rationale for improving our character. Neither God's love nor ours should be sacrificed on that cold altar.

In 1970, a plane crash killed thirty-seven football players and eight coaches from Marshall University in Huntington, West Virginia. They were on their way home from a game in North Carolina. Some players opted to drive home that night instead of fly. A few coaches too. But everyone who boarded the plane died in the crash. Seventy-five people in all. At the time, I was coaching a few miles upstate in Morgantown. I knew the coaches at Marshall, including Rick Tolley, their young head coach. In the early 1960s, when I was an assistant at Florida State and he was a player for Virginia Tech, I coached against him. I also knew many of the Marshall players and their families, having visited in their homes on recruiting trips. News of the crash tore like a shock wave throughout the state. So tragic. So senseless. And for what purpose? To teach a lesson to the surviving widows and orphans? As recompense for their sins? I cannot square such a thought with my experience of the Living God. Yet such suffering causes some to wonder if God cares for us at all, or if God even exists. Memories of the Holocaust are still fresh enough in my memory to appreciate the dark side of the issue. Evil is real. Ugly and painful. At times it is horrid beyond words, and it can fall upon us in measures of breathtaking scope. But my experience through faith assures me of one truth above all others, namely, that God's love trumps evil, suffering, and death.

I will not surrender that conviction. I encourage you not to surrender it, either. I can live with a lot of unanswered questions in life. But I will not live as a defeated man. Evil exists. I cannot make it go away. Neither can you. I will leave it to people smarter than me to argue over why evil exists. The more important issue is how to conquer it. It can be defeated. Faith can make us "more than victorious through Him who loved us" (Rom. 8:37). We may not fully understand the meaning of the darkness, but through faith we can overcome it. Such faith begins by delivering our grief into the hands of the Living God. Christians are a people of the resurrection. God has shown us. Easter is His promise . . . and our assurance.

In 1986, one of my starting linemen at Florida State University was shot to death. His name was Pablo Lopez. The shooting happened on a Friday night, shortly after he broke up a fight outside of a campus dance. The guy he told to leave the party came back a short while later with a shotgun. He aimed the gun at Pablo and pulled the trigger. It happened on a spring break weekend in Tallahassee. Some of the players had gone home to visit their families. Others, such as Pablo, stayed in town because they didn't have the time or money to travel home.

I arrived at the hospital that night and was told that Pablo was dead upon arrival. Word about the shooting had already gone out among the players. A number of them showed up at the emergency room. They knew he was shot, but nothing more. Hospital staff suggested that we meet in the chapel. I gathered the players together and shared the sad news. They were stunned. Some cried out in disbelief. Others leaned into the pews and wept, or else wrapped their arms around teammates in the solidarity that heartache creates. A few stood alone in mute bewilderment. Pablo was with them at football practice just the day before. They had talked with him. Joked around with him. It seemed surreal that they would not see him again. Or that he was dead. How could he be gone? How could it end like that?

I informed the players that I was holding a team meeting that next morning at the football office. I wanted everyone to be there. All who could attend, did. We met in a conference room designed for team meetings. Coaches attended as well. When I walked in, the room was quiet and somber. I recounted the events that led to Pablo's death and told them that Pablo is now in the arms of his Savior. I reminded them that tomorrow is not promised to any of us. Not to Pablo or me or anyone else in the room. I told them that God came in Christ to die for our sins, and that if we have faith in Him, we, too, can have eternal life. God loves each of us, I added, but the decision is left to us. The presence of Pablo's absence put the edge on my words. Life comes down to decisions for all of us. Especially in regard to suffering. Are we merely victims? Or is life meant for more? That answer can only come by making a choice. The God who raised Jesus from the grave is one of our options. Christian faith points us to a way beyond evil and suffering.

Such is what Paul reinforced to the believers who suffered in Rome:

> For if we have been joined with Him in the likeness
> of His death, we will certainly also be in the likeness
> of His resurrection. (Rom. 6:5)

And to those in Corinth whose faith had not yet matured in the face of adversity and death, Paul explained:

> We do not want you to be uniformed, brothers,
> concerning those who are asleep, so that you will
> not grieve like the rest, who have no hope. Since we
> believe that Jesus died and rose again, in the same
> way God will bring with Him those who have fallen
> asleep through Jesus. (1 Thess. 4:13–14)

I think it is critical to realize that suffering has both an outside and an inside dimension. From the outside, the problem of evil and suffering is essentially an intellectual conundrum. The issue is framed along the lines of a math problem. We solve such problems with strict logical thinking. Emotions are not part of the equation. Indeed, they are unhelpful and easily can lead to confusion. When the problem of suffering is viewed strictly from the outside, we are encouraged not to let emotions cloud our thinking. The thinker is to assume a detached, dispassionate, and "objective" point of view. Reason alone is to be our sole guide. When attempting to solve a problem in such a manner, it helps to sit in a comfortable chair and block out all distractions.

Such calm and comfort, however, are precisely what is denied to those who experience evil and suffering from the inside. For them, suffering is not some kind of abstract issue to be contemplated. Suffering is an enemy with whom we fight in a life or death struggle. The problem is anything but theoretical. Suffering is not something that requires meditation and musing; rather, it is a painful and powerful intruder that descends with great force and demands every ounce of our strength in response. Such war is hell. And if we're in it, we fight to win. From the outside, suffering is a classroom debate topic. From the inside, it is an anguishing wrestling match. Hope, joy, and peace are at stake. One's very reason for existence is on the line. You may rest assured that feelings have everything to do with suffering when viewed from the inside. Far from clouding the issue, feelings are precisely what is at stake. One's heart is in the crucible. Those who suffer want a reason to fight the good fight . . . and draw their next breath in hope for what lies beyond the pain. Outcomes must satisfy the heart as well as the mind. Anything less fails to understand the predicament.

In the pages of the Old Testament, the book of Job poignantly depicts the predicament of suffering when viewed as a problem to be resolved from the inside. As the story of Job opens, we are assured that he is a good and righteous man. Yet God allows calamity to fall upon him. First Job loses all his possessions. Then he loses his children in a disastrous accident. Then he loses his health. A lifetime of work and love has been destroyed. Nothing worth having is left to him. Eventually we find Job sitting amidst the burnt-out ruins of his life, dressed in sackcloth and pouring ashes over his head. *Why, O God, why?* is his question to the Almighty. "How could You allow such a thing? What have I done to deserve this misery?" His wife is equally devastated but is long beyond caring about why. "Curse God and be done with it," she cries to her husband. But Job cannot do this. He curses the day he was born, but it seems pointless to curse God. What good would it do? Resentment satisfies nothing. It certainly cannot bring back to him all that he has lost.

Job's friends hear of his demise and come to visit. They sit silently with him for a while, as loving friends often do when there is nothing to say. But eventually they want to do more than merely sit with him in solidarity. So they decide to share their thoughts about what must have gone wrong. All their opinions come down to one thing: "You must have sinned in some way," they tell him. "Otherwise God's wrath would not be turned against you."

Job listens until all of them have spoken. When he no longer can endure their opinions, he politely tells them to take a hike. He has no patience for bad advice. He knows that his friends mean well. But they do not understand what it means to be in his place. Their answers reflect nothing of the truth.

Job's anger continues to burn white hot. He wants to know why God allows such suffering as he has endured. What kind of place is this that God has created? What is the justice of it? Where is the love? He raises his eyes toward an empty sky and pierces it with suffering's demand:

> If only I knew how to find Him,
>   so that I could go to His throne.
> I would plead my case before Him
>   and fill my mouth with arguments.
> I would learn how He would answer me;
>   and understand what He would say to me.
>   (Job 23:3–5)

Then, suddenly, the unexpected happens. Job gets his day in court. The Living God hears his cry and descends from heaven. Clouds darken. The wind begins to howl. God arrives in a frightening whirlwind to give His reply. It's the moment of truth—the moment we might want to stand up and applaud and say, "You go, Job! You've got every right to demand a response from heaven. Put God on the witness stand and hit Him with your questions. Don't let up. Make Him explain. No more what-ifs. No more confusion. No more mystery. We want answers, and we want them now!"

So the Living God comes and gives Job an answer. Only, God's answer is not what Job expects. For the Living God comes with questions of His own. He, too, wants answers.

Listen:

> Then the LORD answered Job from the whirlwind.
> He said:
>
> Who is this who obscures My counsel with ignorant
>   words?
> Get ready to answer me like a man;
>   when I question you, you will inform Me.
> Where were you when I established the earth?
>   Tell Me, if you have understanding.
> Who fixed its dimensions? Certainly you know!
>   Who stretched a measuring line across it?
> What supports its foundations?
>   Or who laid its cornerstone
> while the morning stars sang together
>   and all the sons of God shouted for joy?
>
> Who enclosed the sea behind doors
>   when it burst from the womb,
> when I made the clouds its garment
>   and thick darkness its blanket,
> when I determined its boundaries
>   and put its bars and doors in place,
> when I declared, "You may come this far, but no far-
>   ther; your proud waves stop here"?
> Have you ever in your life commanded the morning,
>   and assigned the dawn its place, so it may seize the
>   edges of the earth, and shake the wicked out of it? . . .

Have you traveled to the sources of the sea
or walked in the depths of the oceans?
Have the gates of death been revealed to you?
Have you seen the gates of deep darkness?
Have you comprehended the extent of the earth?
Tell Me, if you know all this. (Job 38:1, 13,
16–18)

The stark and true answer that comes to Job in the whirlwind
is this: that for all of its good and honest questions, human reason simply cannot encompass the mystery of God. Life's deepest
answers lay just beyond reason's grasp. Reason can lead us in the
direction of truth, even to the threshold, but it cannot force us to
accept the truth to which it points. Emotions stir. Our hearts cry
out. One further step is needed. Confidence in our Creator is the
final step. That's the decision we must make. The Living God is
sovereign, even over our suffering and death. His sovereignty is
our hope. Only in Him can we find peace. In the end we must
trust in His goodness and love. Short of that, there is no deliverance from the pit of despair.

The families of those who died in the Marshall plane crash
suddenly found themselves caught up in a whirlwind. My players who gathered at the hospital the night of Pablo's death, and
who met with me the next morning in the conference room, were
caught up in the same whirlwind. Job cries out to God and finds
himself in a similar whirlwind. The whirlwind is our *cri de cœur*,
our cry from the heart, our impassioned plea. We know so little.
God knows so much. How do we cross that great divide? We seem
to think that all we need in such moments is a good answer, some
response that makes sense to our reasonable questions. But what
we really seek is deliverance. To be delivered from suffering is the

only answer that counts in the end. It is the most powerful answer one can experience.

This is how the psalmist describes suffering's cry from the heart:

> Deep calls to deep in the roar of Your waterfalls; all
> Your breakers and Your billows have swept over me.
> (Ps. 42:7)

The psalmist puts his finger on the heart of the matter. Deep calls out unto deep. In the roar of the waterfalls, we seek a strength to conquer our helplessness and despair. We grope for a saving hand. Deliverance. And for the psalmist, such deliverance comes only from the same mysterious God who allows such waterfalls in the first place. Life ultimately is shrouded in mystery. We do well to grasp that truth up front. Intellect alone is not going to solve our problems. We can never fully understand the darkness. What we need is the overcoming of it.

I am not a theologian or a philosopher. I realize that theodicy is an issue that has challenged many brilliant thinkers over the centuries. They have reached different and contrary conclusions amongst themselves. And they will continue to do so. Reason alone cannot provide the answers we seek. At its core, suffering is not a mind-driven issue but a heart-driven one. The best answers are found from inside of suffering, not outside of it.

I'm reminded of the story about an Irish cop who made a routine traffic stop one day. The motorist, a successful and well-educated attorney, had failed to stop at a stop sign.

"License and registration, please," said the Irishman.

The lawyer decided to talk his way out of the ticket by confusing the patrolman. "Officer," he said, "will you please explain to me the difference between 'slowing down' and 'coming to a complete stop'?"

The Irishman gave him a look and then repeated, "License and registration, please."

"No, seriously," said the lawyer, "I want to know the difference between stop and slow down."

"License and registration, please."

On and on the lawyer quibbled. The Irishman's face grew red with frustration.

Finally, thinking he might have flustered the patrolman and thus gained an edge, the lawyer concluded: "If you will just explain to me the difference between stop and slow down, I'll gladly sign the ticket and pay the fine."

"As you please," said the Irishman. "Step out of the car and I'll explain."

When the lawyer stepped out, the Irishman set upon him, pummeling him with his billy club. As the beating continued, the Irishman asked, "Now, do you want me to stop or just slow down?"

The answers to life's deepest questions are found not on the pages of a dictionary but on the streets of life, not through reason alone but through reason guided by faith. If you want a good reason to believe in God, seek out those who have suffered and come away with a stronger faith in the Living God. Sit down with them. Talk at length. Ask what truths they have learned. Listen with a heart that seeks wisdom. Don't be surprised if their answers sound simple and unsophisticated. They are not. Those who have endured the refiner's fire have had the greatest education of all. Unless you have endured the refiner's fire yourself, you cannot begin to grasp the depth of understanding found in their words of struggle, humility, faith, endurance, hope, and courage. Life's greatest discoveries ultimately come down to truths that are revealed only after we have chosen to believe. Faith leads to understanding, not the other way around. As Fyodor Dostoevsky wrote in *The Brothers Karamazov,* it is not miracles that produce faith but faith that produces miracles.

The message of Scripture is grounded in the personal experience of faith.

> Cast your burden on the LORD, and He will sustain you; He will never allow the righteous to be shaken. (Ps. 55:22)

> The LORD is a refuge for the oppressed, a refuge in times of trouble. (Ps. 9:9)

> God is our refuge and strength, a helper who is always found in times of trouble. (Ps. 46:1)

> No temptation has overtaken you except what is common to humanity. God is faithful, and He will not allow you to be tempted beyond what you are able, but with the temptation He will also provide a way of escape so that you are able to bear it. (1 Cor. 10:13)

> Humble yourselves, therefore, under the mighty hand of God, so that He may exalt you at the

proper time, casting all your care on Him, because
He cares about you. (1 Pet. 5:6–7)

These expressions of faith are not blind and baseless. They are
the voice of reason based on experience. And experience is always
guided by what we are looking to find. A broken twig is never
merely a broken twig. Its brokenness points beyond itself. Faith
leads us toward an answer.

Do not be misled by those who say that God is but a fig-
ment of the imagination. Atheists and agnostics have claimed
that believers do nothing more than imagine God into existence.
Yet they never accuse themselves of having imagined God out of
existence. Sauce for the goose is not applied equally to the gander.
Interesting how that works, isn't it?

All of us are obliged to put our faith in something. Life does
not allow us to be neutral about such matters as love, hate, fidelity, loyalty, justice, and the like. Of that you can rest assured.
Believers and atheists both review the same facts about life and
offer their different interpretations. But which interpretation—
which set of beliefs about the meaning of life—best answers the
deepest questions of the heart?

This is not an idle question. Atheism insists that the universe—and human existence—has no ultimate meaning or purpose. Love ultimately has no purpose. Death has no purpose. Nor
does justice or compassion or loyalty. Suffering, too, is merely a
brute and meaningless fact of life. There's no sense giving hope
to a terminally ill child. No sense asking people to be strong.
Existence is pointless in the end. Such is the faith atheism invites
us to embrace. I wonder sometimes if atheists are just angry children who want someone to blame. That we should believe we

developed into a species that yearns for meaning and purpose in a universe that offers none is more than odd to me. As C. S. Lewis wrote in *Mere Christianity*,

> Creatures are not born with desires unless satisfaction for those desires exists. A baby feels hunger: well, there is such a thing as food. A duckling wants to swim: well, there is such a thing as water. Men feel sexual desire: well, there is such a thing as sex. If I find in myself a desire which no experience in this world can satisfy, the most probable explanation is that I was made for another world. If none of my earthly pleasures satisfy it, that does not prove that the universe is a fraud. Probably earthly pleasures were never meant to satisfy it, but only to arouse it, to suggest the real thing.[1]

Others rail against God by citing atrocities committed in the name of God. The goal of such an argument is to show that the universe is not ruled by a good and loving God. They cite inquisitions, witch hunts, and pogroms, to name a few, and often throw in a mention of the medieval crusades as though it were the *coup de grace*. I've lived long enough to see the folly of such arguments. Scripture's opening pages drive home the message that human nature is flawed by sin. The cross of Christ puts an exclamation point on it. Should it surprise us that sinful humans are capable of sinful acts, regardless of the banner beneath which they march? It shouldn't. To cite human fallibility as compelling evidence against the validity of Christian faith—when Scripture itself insists that all have sinned and fallen short of the glory of God—is a kind of reasoning that baffles me. Shall we also discredit medicine because some doctors do stupid or wicked things? When deep calls out unto deep, it expects a better answer than that.

In this vein, it is instructive to note what happened during the twentieth century when self-avowed atheists grabbed the reins of power. I lived through most of that century. It stands alone as the most brutal century in all of human history. And it introduced us to a scale of death-by-government that simply boggles the mind. I am not talking about deaths that were caused by wars. That is a separate issue entirely. I refer instead to governments that killed their own citizens in the name of a godless ideology.

The most famous atheists of the twentieth century condemned religion as an opiate of the people. Religion does not promote human good, they insisted, but rather perverts it. Hence, they resolved to free people from the shackles of faith and usher in a new secular age . . . one in which God and His teachings were publicly and aggressively repudiated. Theirs would be an age of liberation, we were promised, an epoch of true equality and justice for all. Unaided human reason was to be their only guide. Government power would be the enforcer.

True to their word, they did indeed usher in a new age. They brought us an age unlike any before . . . spawned by an atheist ideology that produced the greatest mega-murderers of all time. Lenin, Stalin, Mao, Pol Pot. And Adolf Hitler too, whose hatred of Jews, gypsies, handicapped, and other minorities was the only reason he needed to murder them.

Soviet communists killed an estimated 100 million of their own people through execution, starvation, and labor camps known as *gulags*. Pause for a moment and let that sink in. Try and imagine your government killing that many people in your own country, not even under the pretense of being at war. Stalin appears to have been the most ruthless of that Soviet gang. Some say over 40 million were killed during his tenure. Mao and his Chinese communist regime annihilated about 75 million of their own citizens up through the Cultural Revolution. In Cambodia, a communist reformer named Pol Pot exterminated approximately one of every four people in his country. His places of mass execution came to be known as "the killing fields." Petty dictators and tyrants in other countries used a similar approach. Genocide in the name of equality and social justice, don't you know? I lived through that era. It was a time of ravaged families . . . mass graves . . . gas chambers . . . prison camps . . . lifeless faces twisted in horror and piles of human bones heaped upon other bones. All those images are still fresh in my mind. Don't think for a minute that it cannot happen again. The twentieth century revealed the depravity that lurks in the human breast. Atheism showcased its own ultimate disregard for the sanctity of life. Theirs is a barren wasteland. I'll take my chances with Jesus of Nazareth. His solutions are better.

I do not believe that suffering and grief are evidence that God does not exist. Or that God does not care. We will never know God as fully as He knows us. We are limited not just physically as human beings but also intellectually. But that doesn't mean we have no evidence of God's steadfast love. Faith opens to us a world of experience and understanding that we cannot get otherwise. If our hearts do not want to believe in God, our heads most assuredly will not make us. But if we seek Him, He will be found. His wisdom comes to us only through trusting Him.

A good example of what I mean is found in marriage. I know my wife loves me. And I love her. We have made our marriage work for over sixty-five years. Such a long life together would not have been possible had we not begun our relationship in an act of faith and maintained that faith in one another through the years. Back in 1948, I believed her love for me was as sincere and committed as my own. I couldn't know that for sure. I had to take it on faith and make a commitment to her. Only then could I discover how loyal and enduring her love could be. Can you imagine what my chances of learning those things about her would have been if, on our wedding day, when asked if I was prepared to love her and stay loyal for the rest of my life, I said, "Well, until I have absolute proof of her trustworthiness and loyalty, I cannot make that promise"?! She would never have tolerated that kind of skepticism. And I would never have known her as well as I do today. A world of knowledge would have been missed. More important, the comfort and joy she brings to my life would never have been possible.

The greatest discoveries in life come after we have made the commitment, not before. Evidence can point us in the right direction, but at some point we must dare to believe. Seek Him and He will be found. Ask expectantly, and He will give us what we need. In moments of grief, He provides an inner assurance that cannot be found elsewhere. He offers not only strength in the midst of suffering but a way beyond suffering, an eternal triumph over it. Such is the wisdom of faith. To all who seek comfort, seek the Living God. Yield your suffering to Him. Trust that He will prove sufficient. Turn over your grief to Him in the confidence that He will make it right. The Living God holds out His strong right hand. We are to take His hand and follow Him.

The Living God dwells in the realm of eternity. That is His home. As Scripture puts it, "But from eternity to eternity the

Lord's faithful love is toward those who fear Him" (Ps. 103:17). Such love has no beginning or end. Moreover, the dwelling place of God is not in some faraway territory. Eternity is here among us. God dwells just as fully in our own cosmic realm as in His own hidden realm. That's a complicated idea, I know. We live in a world of space and time. When an event happens in our world, we look to what caused the event, or to what effects an act will have in the future. We cannot help but think in terms of past, present, and future. But in eternity there is no past or future. For the Living God there is only "now," which includes what we call the past and the future. Past and future are always present events to the Living God. Tomorrow happens to Him today. So does yesterday. God encompasses all of time from His home outside of time. He can respond but once, at a single point in time, and in that one singular act He will have responded to everyone in all periods in time—like a drop of dye spreading through a cup of water.

Scripture tells us the Living God did exactly that two thousand years ago. He entered human history once and for all through Jesus of Nazareth. A single occasion. And that occasion is His definitive response to suffering and death, from the dawn of creation to the end of time.

What is most amazing about the incarnation of God in Christ is that He came among us as a real flesh-and-blood human being. God's incarnation in Jesus was not Kabuki theater. Jesus was not a mirage in which God pretended to act like a human being—pretended to struggle and suffer and die—when in reality it was all a ruse. No. In Jesus of Nazareth, the Living God shows us what is actually possible for human beings through faith in the faithfulness of God. Through Jesus we are shown what faith can mean for all of us.

Jesus is the Living God in human flesh. Yet Jesus knew Himself that same way you and I know ourselves—as a fallible, limited, and conflicted person. He experienced the Living God just as we must, through the eyes of faith. God was the one to whom He prayed, the one He strived to obey and trust. Jesus sought to know and do God's will, the same as we are challenged to do. And Jesus had available to Him the same strength that God offers to all of us. As the author of Hebrews makes clear:

> For we do not have a high priest who is unable to sympathize with our weaknesses, but One who has been tested in every way as we are, yet without sin. (Heb. 4:15)

Scripture tells us that the Incarnation occurred at a time and place in history that was ruled by the Roman Empire. The Living God could have chosen any other place or time. Place and time don't matter when considered from the standpoint of eternity. But He chose Palestine. In the days of Caesar Augustus. And He chose a humble birth.

As historians have pointed out, given the social and political turmoil of that region, it would be difficult for Jesus—or any other person—to remain loyal to the Living God without creating controversy. Jesus discovered this for Himself as His ministry picked up steam. Jesus clearly had a charismatic personality. Much of it had to do with His confidence in God and His singleness of purpose. Be that as it may, multitudes of people soon began to gather wherever He went. Some shouted hosannas. Many asked for His help. A few even called Him Messiah, the Promised One who could break the power of Rome and throw off the yoke of political oppression. Messiah was a poisonous term in Jesus' day. The Roman army ruled over Palestine with an iron fist. And its leaders kept a wary eye on anyone who might try and stir up trouble. They had no patience for civil unrest. They punished it harshly. Local religious leaders feared civil unrest too, but their reasons were different. They feared how Pilate and his Roman soldiers might respond. That may explain why Jesus Himself shied away from having Himself called Messiah. He wasn't looking to create a bloodbath. He had no interest in a political rebellion or blood-tipped swords.

Yet Jesus couldn't help it if people found hope in His message. He couldn't help it that suffering people found comfort and courage and joy in the Living God. Such joy should be found by all, He believed, whether they were society's forgotten people, or frightened civic leaders or haughty Roman overseers. God's love was meant for all of them. He felt compelled to share that good news. Whatever else happened, He believed the word of the Living God must be heard. Of that He was certain. So He pressed on. Many who lived with Him under Roman rule feared the backlash of Jesus' popularity. *For the love of God, what are You trying to do!* But they failed to see the obvious. Everything Jesus did was for the love of God.

By the time Jesus reached Jerusalem on His last visit, His popularity had grown even in the Holy City itself. The buzz about His arrival spread through town. So, too, did the tension that His presence created. It didn't require genius to know that He had enemies. And potential allies. The city was packed with visitors who came to celebrate the Passover Feast. Streets were crowded like a Spring Break weekend, only without the beach. Among the many celebrants were zealous Jewish nationalists.

They resented the Roman occupation of their Holy City. Some were itching for a fight. A populist preacher like Jesus might be just the person to spark a rebellion. I suspect that Jerusalem's civic leaders feared much the same thing. They preferred that Jesus stay away, for good. Even the disciples were anxious. But at least they knew that if trouble broke out, Jesus would get the blame, not them. As for Jesus Himself, He clearly realized the danger He faced. If He remained in town much longer, He probably would not leave town alive. The tension was real . . . and dangerous. On the eve of a great battle, many military commanders over the years have told their men that many of them would be killed in battle the next day. Such news is not a revelation to any soldier on the battlefield. The commander merely is giving a solemn confirmation of what everyone knows, namely, "I may be among those who don't ever see my family again." That's why few men sleep on the night before a battle. Jesus wrestled with the same dreadful thought. Only, in His case, He wasn't surrounded by a bunch of fellow soldiers who would "have His back" if things went wrong. His exposure to danger was much greater. Plus, He didn't carry a weapon. He had no use for one. The battle He fought was not a war against men but a war for God's reign. Weapons made of steel had no place in such an endeavor.

That night, after sharing a meal with His disciples, we are told that Jesus went off by Himself into the Garden of Gethsemane and knelt to pray. He had heard the rumors. Powerful people in Jerusalem were questioning His motives. Some called Him a charlatan. An agent of evil. He could smell the danger. If He went into Jerusalem in the morning, things might spin out of control. Would it be wise to go there? He felt compelled to go, yet He didn't want to. Dread fell upon Him like a heavy yoke. He wanted an alternative. Indeed, He lowered His face to the dirt and prayed that His heavenly Father might make the problem go away. As Matthew tells us:

Going a little farther, He fell facedown and prayed,
"My Father! If it is possible, let this cup pass from
Me." (Matt. 26:39)

It was no small request. Jesus knew exactly what He was asking. Could He own up to His faith? Should He test it to such a degree? Would He man up, even if it meant death? Luke's gospel captures the poignancy of the moment:

Being in anguish, He prayed more fervently, and
His sweat became like drops of blood falling to the
ground. (Luke 22:44)

Show Me a way around this problem, Jesus is saying. *Give Me an alternative.* He's wrestling not so much with God as with Himself. He has to make a decision before He loses control of His destiny. He knows it is not too late. There is still time to cut and run. Maybe He loses face with those who trusted Him. Maybe it means putting the lie to His own convictions. But, hey, nobody's perfect. A lot of good people lie to themselves even when they don't mean to lie. They claim to stand for high principles until loyalty becomes dangerous. Maybe this is just one of those occasions—a live-and-learn moment.

Jesus had helped to create His own dilemma. Through three difficult years He preached faith in the Living God. He proclaimed that God is great; that though we die, yet shall we live. He preached that love is better than hate, mercy is greater than meanness, and giving more rewarding than getting. We should trust God to handle all of our cares, He insisted, and remain loyal in that trust. But a battle now raged within Him. He did not want the suffering that most certainly lay ahead. The worst part of fear is the part of it that we haven't yet experienced. Fear of the unknown is often greater than fear of what we do know. Jesus struggled with those nebulous and frightening uncertainties. Troubling questions roiled within Him. Would He crumble in the face of danger? Was He crumbling even now? Yet, if the faith He preached could not withstand His own inner fears, what good was faith at all? Why was He now wanting God to let this cup pass from Him? Had he been lying to Himself? To everyone? Had the sweet melody of His words seduced them all? Or were His words true and everlasting? There was only one way to find out. He had to stay, not run. He had to see it through. And so He finished His prayer, after what must have been a deep and anguished pause, saying: "Nevertheless, not My will, but Yours, be done" (Luke 22:42). And so the decision was made.

Things unfolded quickly after that. While He was still praying in Gethsemane, His disciple Judas slipped away and reported to authorities that Jesus was alone and ripe for the taking. No one knows for sure what Judas told them, or what his motives were. Maybe he claimed that Jesus was fomenting rebellion. Or that He practiced idolatry. Or stole from the poor. We don't know. But whatever information he shared, he got paid for it, so it must have been worth something. Soldiers showed up not long afterward and arrested Jesus under cover of darkness. He suddenly found Himself swept up into a whirlwind. Life went into fast-forward. His life was no longer in His control. Angry hands yanked Him into an uncertain future. I doubt He could have imagined all that lay ahead.

During the remainder of that exhausting night Jesus was dragged through after-hours court hearings, mocked and jabbed and accused of blasphemy against God. Public reputations were at stake. Questions were thrown at Him. Things only got worse when He refused to tell them what they wanted to hear. A few people hit Him with blows. It's always easy to throw punches when the other guy can't punch back. Some took advantage of the opportunity. Eventually there was nothing left to say or do, except demand His execution. So the first thing that next morning, when the world was awake and back at work, they dragged Him before their Roman overlord, a procurator named Pontius Pilate, and sought his approval to have Jesus put to death. One more dead Jew was not a problem for Pilate. He may have held no grudge against Jesus, but he felt no mercy either. So he agreed. Two other criminals were scheduled to be crucified that day. Jesus was thrown in with them.

Crucifixion was a slow death. Sometimes it took days. Romans liked to make a spectacle of it. They often would line a road with crucified enemies. Such "road kill" helped keep the masses quiet. The execution site in Jerusalem was a craggy bluff called Golgotha, which lay just outside the city walls. From a distance, if you squinted into the sunlight, the jutting rocks looked like a skull. Crosses raised above it climbed dark and angular against the sky. Passersby would get the message.

Before crucifixion, prisoners were tied down and scourged with a whip. Sometimes the leather straps were studded with pieces of bone. Or metal. The purpose was to get prisoners ready for death. Inflict pain. Drain them of hope. Then end their lives slowly. Once you've whipped a few men, you quit thinking of them as persons. It gets easier with time. It becomes a profession, a skill. More about wrist motion than justice. Deserve's got nothing to do with it.

After the scourging, Scripture tells us, Jesus was forced to drag His own crossbeam to the site of His execution. The other two prisoners must have done the same. It was all part of the spectacle. Christian history remembers this death march as the *Via Dolorosa*, the pathway of sorrow. Many had to walk it on their way to crucifixion. Jesus now found Himself among them. Harsh voices shouted at Him to keep moving. Cruel hands shoved Him toward a place of agony. An incredible lightness of being must have swarmed in His brain like bees in a frenzy. We are told that He stumbled and fell. A man from among the crowd was forced to step in and carry His cross the rest of the way. His name was Simon. I do not know if He and Jesus exchanged words. I don't even know if Jesus noticed Him. The world must have been a blur at that moment.

The gospel of Mark tells us that in the sixth hour of His crucifixion, as He neared the moment of death, Jesus let out a loud and mournful cry. For those who affirm the divinity of Jesus but give scant thought to His humanity, what Jesus says in His dying breath must sound all wrong. *"Eloi, Eloi, lemá sabachtháni? . . . My God, My God, why have You forsaken Me?"* (15:34).

It is a godforsaken cry. The helpless cry of someone abandoned to a disillusionment worse than death. Was there anger in His voice? Resentment? A sense of having been betrayed? Or was He merely dying and afraid? I was not there. I do not know. But when I consider the experience of suffering from the inside rather than from the outside, the mystery of Jesus' cry of abandonment becomes less opaque. All I need to do is think about what happens when any of us suffers so deeply.

In earlier days, Jesus had referred to God as *Abba*, Father. It's the word He used when He taught His disciples to pray: "Our [Abba] Father in heaven, Your name be honored as holy" (Matt. 6:9). *Abba* is a personal term. Jesus used it frequently in the period before His trip to Jerusalem. It reflected His deep bond with His heavenly Father, the kindred spirit that arises whenever we take up someone's cause and give all we have for their sake. That is what His heavenly Father meant to Him. He tasted the power of the Father. He saw what the Father was doing through Him. He wanted His disciples to have the same experience. He wanted them filled with God's infinite and unconquerable love. But where had such faith now left Him? Jesus finds Himself alone, in pain, and dying on a cross. The Jewish Holocaust, anyone? The grieving families of tsunami victims? The parents whose child is dying from leukemia? Where does faith get us in the end?

"Eloi," He calls out with what strength is still in Him. Not *"Abba*, My Father," like in earlier days, but *"Eloi*, My God," a more generic term. We can see what has changed. The personal dimension is missing. There's a distance between them now that He doesn't understand. It's as if *Abba* has chosen to back away, has lost interest in Jesus' life precisely at the moment Jesus needs Him most. "Deep calls to deep in the roar of Your waterfalls," the psalmist wrote. *Why, O God, why?* so many Holocaust victims screamed. Jesus now finds Himself in that same dark pit. His experience is no less real simply because we call Him our Savior. He experienced suffering as any of us do. He was in all ways like us. And His cry from the cross was just as anguished and dreadful

as any that can fall from our lips when faith seems to have failed us: "My God, My God, why have You forsaken Me?"

On Easter morning, three days after Jesus died, deep answered unto deep. *Why, O God, why?* was answered. And Jesus' own forlorn cry was answered. The Living God stepped from behind the veil of eternity to answer that question once . . . and decisively . . . and for all time. He answered from the inside of suffering, not from the outside. The resurrection of Jesus is His answer.

He showed that evil and suffering hold no power in His eternal domain. He showed that evil and suffering hold no final power over us. And He showed that evil and suffering have never possessed the power to thwart His plan for creation. Not in the past. Not in the present. And not in the future.

The Living God says,

> Behold, hear Me with fear and trembling. I am
> the Lord God Your Creator. I am from Everlasting
> to Everlasting. You were not here when I created
> the firmament and cast stars across the heavens.
> You were not around when I created the dawn and
> caused life to come forth. Even greater things than
> these I have done, things that remain hidden from
> your eyes. You know so little of My ways. But I have
> shown you what you need to know. I am your Creator and Redeemer. I have called you by name. You
> are Mine. Fear not. For where I am, there you shall
> be also. The resurrection is My sign to you . . . and
> My promise.

I believe in the resurrection of Jesus.

The Living God is my refuge and my hope. He is the Sovereign God of all that is. My Creator and my Redeemer. So I put my life in His safekeeping. My cares are in His hands.

Such is the wisdom of suffering.

Note
1. C. S. Lewis, *Mere Christianity* (Harper Collins, 2001).

CHAPTER 10

THE WISDOM
of LOVE

Guard your heart above all else, for it is the source of life.
(Prov. 4:23)

Many years ago I recruited an All-American high school prospect from another state. He was a "can't miss" player at the college level. He stood 6'5" and weighed 265 pounds, which was huge at the time. His body was harder than a Greek statue, his legs and arms corded with muscle. I was excited when he signed a scholarship and arrived on campus that fall.

College rules in those days didn't allow freshmen to play on the varsity. He had to sit out that first year. But I was confident he would be a starter by his sophomore year and earn All-American honors by the end of the season. Sure enough, we put him in the starting lineup for the first game that next year. When we reviewed game film the next day, the other coaches and I noticed he didn't play nearly as well as we expected. After the second game, we reviewed film again. He played worse than the week before. I blamed myself for his poor performance. I rushed him, I figured, throwing him into the starting lineup before he had a chance to learn our system. We demoted him to second string. His replacement was only 205 pounds, not nearly as big as we needed for linemen, but the kid was a fighter. What he lacked in stature, he made up for in tenacity. That kid ended up starting for us the remainder of the year. The next year rolled around and I expected my prospective All-American to have a breakout year. He understood our system and had a good grasp of his assignments. I was excited to see what he could do. Yet, once again, I was disappointed. He got beat out in practice by yet another guy who was smaller and less talented. For the rest of his junior year he played a backup role, never able to break into the starting lineup.

The next year—his senior season—our team was going through spring training. Scouts from various NFL teams visited college campuses each spring to watch practice and eyeball some of the pro prospects. The scouts normally came to my office first, asking which players they should keep an eye on. I would give them a list of players I thought might succeed at the next level.

One of the scouts was on the field with me at practice that spring. A group of linemen ran past us. As he watched them jog by, the pro scout made a whistling sound, like one might do after finding a piece of buried treasure. "Who is that?!" he asked. His eyes were locked onto my prospective All-American. He held out the list I had given him and asked which one he was.

"He's not on the list," I told him.

"Not on the list? Is he too young?"

"No. He's a senior."

"Is he injured?"

"No injuries," I replied.

"Personal problems?"

"Nope. None that I know of."

"Then why did you leave him off the list?"

"Because he just doesn't have it," I answered.

The little 205-pound player who beat him out for a starting job certainly had it—that intangible quality every coach looks for. But my all-world athlete didn't have it. I don't mean to imply that he was not a fine young man. I never had problems with him. But to build a football team, you need players who have *it*.

It transcends physique. Little guys can have more of it than big guys. *It* is not tied to personality or intellect. *It* is not reducible to brute strength, either. To this day, I cannot boil *it* down to a single word. *Tenacity? Courage? Strength? Determination? Enthusiasm? Intensity? Resolve?* I'm not sure what single word best captures it. But if you spend much time around athletes in practice, you will soon discover which players have *it* and which ones don't. They possess an inner drive to give the best they have. They practice longer, work harder, and accomplish more than other players of equal ability. I've watched them take *it* with them beyond football to develop fine families and successful work careers. Some were quiet. Some were flamboyant. Some made lots of money. Some made little. But *it* showed in almost everything they did.

In this particular case the scout didn't believe me. He saw what I had seen three years earlier—the imposing stature, the angular torso, the muscular legs and arms. Moreover, he felt confident that his staff of professional coaches could develop this player into a fine pro athlete. They drafted him that next year. He lasted only two weeks. Then they cut him from the team.

Scripture associates *it* with one particular organ in the body—namely, the heart. But *heart* doesn't mean the actual physical organ. Heart is a metaphor for our deepest and innermost self. It includes the body but is also more than the body. Heart is the wellspring of thought and passion . . . the fount of all human endeavor. How shall we live our lives? With what intensity? By what standards and toward what end? Only the heart can decide.

Hence, Scripture admonishes:

> Guard your heart above all else, for it is the source of life. (Prov. 4:23)

> For as he thinks in his heart, so is he. (Prov. 23:7 NKJV)

In that same vein the psalmist cries out to God, saying:

> God, create a clean heart for me and renew a steadfast spirit within me. (Ps. 51:10)

A great many verses of Scripture allude to the heart as the place where all of life's great decisions are made. Life, in essence, is an affair of the heart.

An intelligent heart acquires knowledge, and the ear of the wise seeks knowledge. (Prov. 18:15 esv)

The heart of him who has understanding seeks knowledge, but the mouths of fools feed on folly. (Prov. 15:14 esv)

My son, don't forget my teaching, but let your heart keep my commands; for they will bring you many days, a full life, and well-being. Never let loyalty and faithfulness leave you. Tie them around your neck; write them on the tablet of your heart. Then you will find favor and high regard in the sight of God and man. Trust in the Lord with all your heart, and do not rely on your own understanding. (Prov. 3:1–5)

My son, if you accept my words and store up my commands within you, listening closely to wisdom and directing your heart to understanding; further- more, if you call out to insight and lift your voice to understanding, if you seek it like silver and search for it like hidden treasure, then you will understand the fear of the Lord and discover the knowledge of God. (Prov. 2:1–5)

For the word of God is living and effective and sharper than any double-edged sword, . . . able to judge the ideas and thoughts of the heart. (Heb. 4:12)

Scripture can also speak of *heart* and *soul* synonymously, as two ways of talking about the same person.

> For wisdom will enter your heart, and knowledge
> will be pleasant to your soul. (Prov. 2:10 NIV)

> "Only take care, and keep your soul diligently, lest
> you forget the things that your eyes have seen, and
> lest they depart from your heart all the days of your
> life." (Deut. 4:9 ESV)

It's interesting to me how we retain these notions of heart and soul in some of our most common idioms. When a person shies away from a difficult challenge, we say "his heart isn't in it" or that "he doesn't have the heart for it," or perhaps that he is "faint of heart." Likewise, a heartfelt tune can be referred to as "soul music." A person can be admonished either to "search your heart" or to "do some soul searching." Indeed, we accuse heartless people of "not having a soul" and soulless people of "not having a heart."

I suspect we make these associations with the heart—the central organ in our chest area—for the same reason the ancient Hebrews did, namely, life's deepest experiences are felt in that general physical region. We talk today about the brain as the center of emotion and thought, for all the obvious scientific reasons, but we don't experience life between our ears in any ways that are passionate. Think for a minute about how we actually experience certain emotions. Guilt, anxiety, longing, and remorse arise in the chest and can extend to the abdomen. The piercing stab of betrayal—especially by a lover—is felt most intensely in that same physical area. Every young guy knows what it's like to feel gut sick when his girlfriend breaks up with him. At the other end of the emotional spectrum, the flowering of puppy love and the euphoria of newfound romance are chest-pounding experiences. Who hasn't felt their hearts soar and threaten to explode with joy when the "perfect person" appears? Pride of achievement is felt there, also. Chests tend to feel swollen when the crowd chants our name for some feat we accomplished. Mercy, pity, compassion, charity, and parental pride are heartfelt too. Awe and dread can start in the chest or abdomen and quickly spread like a shock wave throughout the body. Abject fear roils in the lower abdomen.

My point is that our deepest and most meaningful experiences are psychosomatic. They seem to manifest themselves most poignantly in the center of our bodies, but at a depth that fingers cannot reach. I've seen grown men, wracked with grief, curl up and clutch their stomachs, trying to get their arms around the pain. I've seen mothers tremble and lose the strength of their legs upon hearing tragic news, others grab their chest in wonder or fall slump-shouldered beneath the weight of failure or sin. Life at its most intense is experienced bone deep . . . down in the core of our souls . . . that region we speak of as the heart. At its worst—and best—life is a heartfelt experience.

Faith itself is a bone-deep experience. When God says He wants your heart, it means He wants your whole self. He wants your complete commitment. Your deepest loyalty. Your best effort. If your heart is not in it, you are not in it. Your heart is *you*, the person who chooses how you will live and who you will be. From the heart flow the issues of life.

Have that in mind as you read these powerful words from Deuteronomy:

"Listen, Israel: The LORD our God, the LORD is
One. Love the LORD your God with all your heart,
with all your soul, and with all your strength. These
words that I am giving you today are to be in your
heart." (Deut. 6:4–6)

Do you see what He is saying? Not that we are composed
of three different parts—heart, soul, and strength—but that we
are to love the Lord our God with our whole selves, unreserved,
with everything we have at our disposal. To love with heart, soul,
and strength means to obey God's will and follow His path with
everything we've got in us to give. How can a football player be
good if he holds back or quits before the play is over? He will
never know how good he can be—and we coaches will never
know—until he gives all he's got. If he doesn't have the heart for
it, we'll need to find someone who does. In a similar manner, how
can any of us discover what life is meant to be until our hearts are
obedient to the One who created us?

Notice in the quote from Deuteronomy that love is commanded. That is a clear indication of how the Scripture understands love. Love is primarily an action, not a feeling. Feelings are
always involved, but feelings cannot be commanded. Actions can.
Love is a commitment to a way of life. More specifically, love is
the pattern of life we embrace when our hearts are committed to
God. It is a curiosity of loving behavior that the more we practice
it, the more certain feelings take root in our lives and begin to
flourish.

When I started out in football, we never heard a coach talk
about loving one another. Love was for sissies and Sunday school.
The coach wanted us tough and nasty. He might grab a player by

the jersey and yell at him to "get out there and hurt somebody . . . hit 'em hard . . . bloody some noses . . . kill 'em . . . make 'em pay." And that was just at practice against our own team-mates! It helps to understand that many of the players on my team had just returned from the battlefields of World War II. We had guys on the team in their late twenties and early thirties. Wartime expressions were meant to motivate them. Not that they needed any motivation. We wore leather helmets in those days. Facemasks had not yet been invented. Moreover, the padding in our uniforms was thin and the rulebook was thinner. Contusions, sprains, twisted joints, broken noses, and bloody lips were part of the game. Indeed, they were badges of honor. Guys without some blood on their jersey were suspected of being slackers. Some of the seasoned military vets on the team introduced blocking and tackling techniques that young freshmen like me had never seen before. These skills were usually demonstrated when the referee's head was turned. You never, ever, wanted to be on the bottom of a big pile-up after a tackle. You might get a stab in the eye, a broken finger, or a bite on the arm. Football was a different kind of game in those days.

These days, coaches preach quite a bit about the importance of players loving one another. They speak openly about the bond of love they share with players and coaches alike. They have learned—as we all eventually do—that even in arenas such as coaching and building a successful team, love is required. Genuine love. Sacrificial and heartfelt. Players come together as a team when they put their teammates first. Selfishness loses games. Selflessness wins. A young man will make sacrifices when he sees how his sacrifice helps others. Coaches will too. Showing love gives rise to an emotional bond that is difficult to break. I coached long enough to see what genuine love can accomplish even in a game. If you want to build a winning team, build upon love. Don't just talk about love. *Do* love. *Show* love. *Practice* love. Regularly. You will be amazed at what happens next.

Let me illustrate. When I coached at FSU, we took our team to a hotel out of town on the Friday before each home game. We wanted the players away from distractions. The time was spent eating, holding position meetings, going over game plans, and relaxing in preparation for the next day's game. Toward the end of the evening I would get the team together and lead a devotion. I used this occasion to remind players that life is about much more than football. I wanted them to think about the future and where they planned to spend eternity. Toward the end of the meeting, players were invited to share some personal details about themselves. The goal was not to push Christian faith upon them, or to have them push their faith upon others. Rather, I would go to one or two players in advance and ask if they would mind telling us about themselves at the end of the devotional—just some personal details about their lives that they thought others might want to know.

The occasions were often lighthearted and funny. The guys certainly knew one another well enough already. But you would be amazed at some of the stories we heard. I think of one particular player who I stayed on pretty hard in practice. He was a great athlete, but not as great as I thought he could be. He never took practice as seriously as I wanted, joking and kidding around between plays rather than staying focused. So I tended to criticize him a lot for lack of effort. When he volunteered to speak at one of those Friday night devotionals, he stood up and told about the day in his childhood when he walked home and found his mother shot dead on the kitchen floor. He never knew his father. I began to understand why he might not think of football the same way I did. I came to love him differently after that—with more depth, for sure—and in a way more fitting to the truth about his life and mine.

Another player talked about his own difficult childhood years. His mother was heavily addicted to drugs and his father was off in prison. He was sent to live with his grandmother. She loved and cared for him during those difficult times, but she died when he was fourteen. With no one around to support him, he was sent out of state to live with some relatives, but that didn't work out. So he moved back to his home state and lived with other relatives, but that didn't work out either. On his own he returned to his home-town, lived alone in an abandoned building, enrolled himself in high school, and joined the football team. He basically took care of himself as best he could. To make ends meet, he sometimes did things he shouldn't do. There had never been a helpful male role model in his life, much less a sense of security and belonging. His high school coach eventually learned about the situation. The coach discussed it with his minister. With the church's support and the coach's encouragement, the player eventually moved in and lived with the coach's family. We recruited him to FSU a few years later. His story touched a great many players that night at the devotional.

Love arises not simply in feelings but also in seeing the world as it really is. That's when love is most needed. Love is nice when we're in the mood for it. Love works best, however, when we see the world for what it is and then do what love requires. I can assure you that players play hard for people they know and love. They will make sacrifices when they see how their sacrifices help others. Do you want players to play with all their heart, soul, and strength? Give them a reason greater than themselves. A reason rooted in love . . . and truth. Show them how. Then get out of the way.

Spiritual love—the foundation of all expressions of love—is rooted in relationships. Not all relationships are equal. What we owe to one person we may not owe to another. A parent's obligation to a child is quite different from what is owed to a neighbor or stranger. But how do we decide what is owed to whom, and in what measure? Scripture teaches that our relationship with the Living God is our one sure guide. Our relationship to Him transcends all others. We are to love the Lord our God with all our heart, soul, and strength. Only then will we best know how to love others and be loved ourselves. I have written of that experience frequently in the pages of this book. Wisdom begins in the fear of the Lord. Otherwise we flounder, awash in conflicting desires and obligations without any real sense of direction. If we are in right relationship with God, we then can know how best to love others. With God as our guide, we know what to hope for from others and what we owe them ourselves. Love becomes the imitation of God's love for us.

When we think of love as wholehearted commitment to the Living God, we clear up a lot of confusion about love. Even an old coach like me can make sense of love as Scripture defines it. No one in their right mind would ever ask me to write an advice column for those in search of "true love" and "real romance." I lack the requisite delicacy. But if asked, I have an idea of what I'd write. I would write it only once, then have it reprinted each day:

Dear Lost and Lovelorn,

It isn't all about you, even though you think it is. So first thing, get your head screwed on right. Forget yourself and you have a chance of finding yourself. Love God and you will find love, more love than you deserve and in more ways than you imagine. But you won't find the treasure without the map. Any good pirate can tell you that. God owns the map to the treasure you seek. So seek God first. And be advised: the treasure is worth much more than you imagine.

Resolve to do God's will first and always. Keep that always in mind. If it is romantic love you seek, first get acquainted with what love is all about. Resolve to be loving with everyone you meet. Love others the way you think God wants you to love them. Try it with family members. Then a friend. Then a colleague or stranger. And then with people you don't like. That last one will come in handy if you ever get married.

Practice love regularly, not just once or twice, and resolve to do it even when you don't want to. Get a feel for what to expect. The results won't always be to your liking, but most often they will be. There is no substitute for experience. So practice, practice, practice. Once you know what you are able to give—freely and in obedience to God—you will know what to look for in a lifelong companion.

Otherwise, get a dog.

We fall into a trap when we start thinking that love is a feeling. Love always comes attached to feelings, but feelings are emotions that happen to us. They come and go—or else their intensity ebbs and flows—based on circumstances beyond our control. Feelings cannot be ginned up at will. Were it otherwise, we could end a lot of human misery simply by visiting a funeral home and telling everyone not to be sad. Can you imagine standing at the altar and pledging that you will love, honor, cherish, and serve your beloved for as long as you *feel* like it? Try that one on your fiancée and I imagine she will wallop you with all her heart, soul, and strength—a punch of biblical proportions.

Romance novelists and Hollywood screenwriters have gone a long way toward convincing us that true love is fundamentally a feeling—a sensuous and enchanting feeling—that just happens when we meet the right person. In my day you saw it in movies such as *An Affair to Remember* and *Sabrina*. These days it's *You've Got Mail* and *Sleepless in Seattle*. There's nothing wrong with dreaming about the movie experience. But in reality, such movies say more about our insecurities, loneliness, and yearning for affection—usually to the tune of some smarmy background music—than they do about the reliability of our hearts.

Don't get me wrong. Romance is wonderful. Most all of us feel bathed by grace when such moments arise. I fell head-over-heels in love with my wife Ann when I was still a teenager. And she fell in love with me. We wouldn't have married had we not been so attracted to one another. Of course, hormones play a big role when you're a teenager. Later in life, other needs come into play. And they come attached to powerful emotions. What's not to love about someone who insists you are perfect in every way? Someone who claims your flaws are cute and your blind spots are mere idiosyncrasies? Someone who laughs at your jokes, shows you off to their friends, stares at you in rapt wonder, tells you repeatedly how smart and talented you are, and can't understand why anyone could find you hard to get along with? And I haven't even gotten to the physical attraction. Ah, the majesty of passionate romance. The intoxicating joy. Two star-crossed lovers, glowing with supernatural radiance, convinced that eternity was made just for them. If only it would never change. But, alas, it does. Pixie dust comes with a time stamp.

Real love is complex and ever-changing. Many of its demands cannot be anticipated. Great wisdom is required. Such wisdom comes only from God. "Love the LORD your God with all your heart, with all your soul, and with all your strength," Deuteronomy 6:5 tells us. Do that and love can adapt and flourish. Lose sight of that and you lose sight of love.

Wanting to be loved is the most natural feeling in life. I believe in happy endings. That's why I'm a Christian. But some people are addicted to the feeling of romantic or sensual love in ways that are not healthy or wise. They turn to it for the mood-altering feeling it provides. They experience love more as a drug than a commitment . . . a means of finding relief from insecurity, emptiness, and lack of self-esteem. They enjoy the new relationship as long as the medication lasts. But as it wears off, their loyalty fades. Having spent over half a century on a college campus, I have seen this phenomenon occur often. I've seen it in older adults as well. They want the movie version of love, right up to the point when the credits begin to roll. But what happens after the movie is over and the lights come on? One or the other of our star-struck lovers wakes up to a consolation prize who bears little resemblance to the person they fell in love with. Then it's time to move on. Love addicts get disappointed a lot. And bitter. "You're not the person I thought you were!" shouts the angry love junkie. And they are right. Only, after shouting that they obviously *weren't thinking* when they fell in love with you, you nonetheless get blamed for their lack of thinking skills. Go figure. The alternative history for love addicts is to stay in the relationship for as long as they can, albeit with great disappointment and unhappiness, drifting away from time to time, flirting and having affairs, anything it takes to self-medicate.

Love is not something one can *fall into* or gin up at will. Feelings happen. Love is a choice. Love seizes whatever feelings are at hand and reshapes them according to love's purpose. That purpose is always greater than us. It is even greater than the things we love. The best feelings we can ever have are feelings that have been shaped by obedience to God. God doesn't just know love. God *is* love. I recruited many talented football players. Many of them came in knowing they were good. And they were right. But I knew ways to make them better. Those who are coachable have a bright future. Those who aren't usually end up on the bench. God knows how He intended us to feel about one another. If we learn to love Him, He will teach us how to love others. Powerful and satisfying emotions come attached to such knowledge. God introduces us to a different dimension.

When I was a young man, I ran track as well as played football and baseball. There is a unique phenomenon many runners experience called "the runner's high." Distance runners know what I mean. Somewhere in the process of an extended and intense run, a mind-altering and mood-altering transformation occurs. Sometimes it occurs when one feels near the point of collapse. Suddenly the heart rate slows down. Breathing becomes calm.

Pain dissipates. A peaceful and relaxed mood sets in. Some even find it euphoric. You suddenly feel as though you could run forever. The body's exhaustion seems to melt away.

People who regularly engage in strenuous and intense exercise—from running to weight lifting to mountain biking—have experienced the "high" I'm talking about. It's quite similar to the thrill of romance, only without the drama and financial outlay. The precondition, however, is regular and intense exercise. It's definitely not something that happens by accident. You can't jog around the block once a week and expect to enter that zone. Or do an occasional bicep curl while chatting with friends at the gym. Up until recently, many people scoffed at the notion of a runner's high and called it a myth. "Show me the evidence," they said. "Show me how such a thing can happen." And sure enough, some researchers from Germany finally did show them. We now know the experience is genuine. Medical research has shown that endorphins can build up in the blood system and suddenly flood into the brain, creating the relaxed, mood-altering experience known as "the runner's high."

Scripture tells of an analogous experience among believers. The experience is called *salvation*. It is more than mood-altering. It is also *life-changing*. What changes is our way of living. We live to imitate God as we know Him in Jesus Christ. Along with this new life comes a flourishing of emotion, the kind of emotion that only love can nourish. Being saved is not about belting out gospel hymns or flogging oneself in public. It is not about kissing snakes or shouting jeremiads or being meek and milquetoast as a lamb. Salvation is more about courage, fortitude, strength, trust, endurance, integrity, patience, kindness, mercy, and the passions that go with them.

Love is just as masculine as it is feminine. No guy can truly be a "man's man" if he runs like a coward from the demands of God. Love requires courage and strength just as much as tenderness and long-suffering. Ultimately, love is not masculine or feminine. Love is God. And because God created us in His image, love is human as well as divine. Love is the supreme character of God and the key to our own humanity. To know God is to love, and to love is to know ourselves. Anything less leads to inhumanity. Every act of unloving is a sin against ourselves. In loving, we find the life God intended us to have all along.

The "runner's high" that the saved have experienced is an inner peace that seems to pass all understanding. The saved live for what lies beyond the horizon. Something powerful. Life-changing. It is love, pure and simple. A love that gives rest to our restless hearts. Those who find it—and who, in turn, imitate it—taste love on earth as it is in heaven.

Perhaps love's most well-known and oft-quoted passage in Scripture is Paul's instruction to believers in Corinth. The passage is frequently recited in marriage ceremonies. It is most properly applied, however, to all of one's life and all of one's relationships. Listen with ears to hear:

> If I speak human or angelic languages but do not
> have love, I am a sounding gong or a clanging cym-
> bal. If I have the gift of prophecy and understand all
> mysteries and all knowledge, and if I have all faith
> so that I can move mountains but do not have love,
> I am nothing. And if I donate all my goods to feed
> the poor, and if I give my body in order to boast but
> do not have love, I gain nothing. Love is patient,
> love is kind. Love does not envy, is not boastful, is

not conceited, does not act improperly, is not self-ish, is not provoked, and does not keep a record of wrongs. Love finds no joy in unrighteousness but rejoices in the truth. It bears all things, believes all things, hopes all things, endures all things. Love never ends. But as for prophecies, they will come to an end; as for languages, they will cease; as for knowledge, it will come to an end. For we know in part, and we prophesy in part. But when the perfect comes, the partial will come to an end. When I was a child, I spoke like a child, I thought like a child, I reasoned like a child. When I became a man, I put aside childish things. For now we see indistinctly, as in a mirror, but then face to face. Now I know in part, but then I will know fully, as I am fully known. Now these three remain: faith, hope, and love. But the greatest of these is love. (1 Cor. 13:1–13)

We should not so much marvel at Scripture as yearn to write it ourselves.

All knowledge comes through grace from the Living God.

The wise understand.

Fools do not.

I thank You, O God, that my restless soul finds rest in You. What I do not deserve, You give me anyway. Your love is grace. It humbles me. And fills me. Now strengthen me to love others as You have loved me. Gird me for battle. Make me strong. For only in loving do I find a wisdom that sets me free.

EPILOGUE

I am sure of this, that He who started
a good work in you will carry it on to
completion until the day of Christ Jesus.
(Phil. 1:6)

I enjoyed playing sports in college. In addition to football I ran track and played baseball each spring. My final season was in 1952.

As we entered the final few games of the baseball season that year, I was the only player on the team without a home run. Everyone else had at least one. But not me. I was more a lead-off hitter than a power guy. My best shots were hard line drives. Try though I did, I simply had not been able to hit one out of the park.

As everyone knows, a home run is the supreme batting achievement. Singles are nice. Doubles and triples are better. But home runs are king. Who hasn't heard of Barry Bonds, Babe Ruth, Hank Aaron, and A-Rod? Even at the college level, fans like to hear that crack of the bat and watch the ball sail high and far until it disappears over the wall. Such hits bestow a mythical status like no other. It's much the same at the college level. Hitting a homer is a big deal. Not only do you score a run with a single swing, but you also get to trot leisurely around the bases while the crowd applauds. The good home run hitters don't even act like it's a big deal. They shrug it off as if to say, *Yeah, it's the kind of thing I'm likely to do anytime I step to the plate.* I wanted to experience that for myself.

Then it happened.

I don't recall who it was we played. It was a late season game at our own ballpark, so I assume it was the second meeting in a home-and-away series.

Anyway, when it was my turn to bat, I swung on a fastball and drove it past the shortstop toward a gap in centerfield. I knew the ball was hit well the second it cracked off the bat. I threw the bat aside and dashed for first base. As I closed in, the first-base coach pointed toward second and yelled for me to keep going. I planted my foot and made a hard left turn, glancing to the outfield as I ran. The ball was rolling toward the fence with two players in hot pursuit. Everything happened quickly after that. Seeing I might get one more base, I rounded second and sprinted for third. I rose up as I neared the bag, preparing to slide feet-first. I glanced at my third base coach. He was on the sideline just beyond the bag. Palms down would mean *slide.* Palms toward me meant *come in standing.* I was looking for the signal. But the coach wasn't looking at me. His eyes were on the outfield. He suddenly began swinging his arm in a wide circular motion—the signal for me to turn and head for home plate. "Go! . . . Go! . . . Go!" he yelled. So with only a slight break in stride I stabbed my foot against third base and pushed toward home. As I made the turn I heard him shout, "You better hurry!" That wasn't the boost of confidence I was hoping for. This one would be close.

As I sprinted those last few yards, I saw how the finish would end. The catcher had moved into position on the third-base line, about three feet out from home plate. His goal was to block my access. He squatted down with a slight lean in my direction. His left hand was on the ground for balance. The other was angled toward the outfield. He opened the catcher's mitt. Obviously the throw was on its way. I could hear players and fans shouting, but it was white noise, the kind of background sound that confirms drama but doesn't interfere. My focus condensed into a single point-instant of purpose. *Score.* Nothing else. Just, *score.* He was a bigger man than me, stocky and with thick shoulders, planted in my path like the stump of an old oak. But I was at full sprint. Inertia was my equalizer. As I closed within a few steps, I lowered my shoulder. Collision was inevitable. My head turned slightly on the next step, more for protection than anything, and with the third came impact. He went sprawling onto his back. I came down on top of him at an angle.

The sensation of plowing into another man's body is not like hitting a brick wall. The pain is different. Bodies are pliable. The impact is like slamming into a hard rubber mat that gives way in some places but not others. You feel it in your bones, but the jolt is different. The sounds are different too. More personal.

I quickly regained my sensibilities and spotted home plate less than two feet away. Scrambling over the catcher, I stretched out my arm and made contact. The home plate umpire was standing near my hand. "Safe!" he yelled. And with that I realized I had finally done it! A home run. Yes, an inside-the-park homer rather than a blast over the outfield wall, but a home run nonetheless.

I got to my feet and looked around. The ball lay in the dirt beside the catcher. Whether it came out of his mitt on contact or bounced into us afterwards, I no longer recall. I never saw it come in because my head was turned the other way.

I dusted off my shirt and jogged toward the dugout. Teammates streamed out to congratulate me. I went down the line shaking hands with each of them. We didn't know about fist-bumps back in 1952. Handshakes and "attaboys" were the standard of the day. Man alive, did the accolades feel good. And I now could hear the white noise for what it was—happy fans acknowledging my feat.

Before the handshakes ended, I heard the first-baseman yelling. I glanced over. "Throw it to me," he hollered. I turned and saw the catcher pick up the ball. "Throw it here!" the first baseman repeated. The catcher tossed him the ball. As we stared in confusion, the first baseman caught the ball and stepped on the bag at first base.

"Out!" yelled the first-base umpire. He jabbed his thumb in the air for emphasis.

"What do you mean 'out'?" we said.

"Runner never touched first," he replied.

And so ended my one good chance for a home run. All the effort—including my heroics at home plate—counted for nothing. Teammates tried to console me. One claimed the umpire got it wrong. Others nodded in agreement. Friends are good about withholding the truth when it might hurt too much. They were too kind to point out that *somebody* blew his only home run by failing to touch first base. But, alas, that *somebody* was me.

I think of that game when I reflect on the wisdom of faith. The lesson is simple.

Second base represents all the good things we do in life, the commitments we make, and energies we give to make our lives worth living. We intend for our "at bat" to get us somewhere important, so we hustle from one base to the next, our minds set on reaching home plate.

Third base represents the honors and recognition we receive along the way. The world honors us for many things: our money, our success, the records we amass, and the trophies we've earned. The world's applause seems like a sign that we are on our way somewhere important.

Home plate, of course, represents heaven, the destination we strain to achieve because it's the one award we want most of all. We want our lives to matter not just on this side of death but on the other side as well. And so we lower our heads and bull forward toward the finish line, confident that we can score.

But all our efforts come to nothing if we have failed to do the one most important thing for any base runner—namely, touch first base. Failing that, the rest of the journey is futile. Jesus Christ *is* first base.

> "I am the way, the truth, and the life. No one comes
> to the Father except through Me." (John 14:6)

If we do not touch first, the rest is nullified.